Returning

Stories from the Indianapolis Senior Center

Edited by Shari Wagner

Writers' Center of Indiana
Orders, information, reprint permissions:
P.O. Box 30507
Indianapolis, IN 46230-0707
317-255-0710
mail@indianawriters.org
www.indianawriters.org

Returning:
Stories from the Indianapolis
Senior Center
Edited by Shari Wagner

Copyright © 2012 INwords, The Writers' Center of Indiana
All rights reserved
ISBN: 978-0-9849501-1-9

Returning

Stories from the Indianapolis Senior Center

Edited by Shari Wagner

The Writers' Center of Indiana

With Special Thanks To:

SUPPORTED BY THE ARTS COUNCIL AND THE CITY OF INDIANAPOLIS

CENTRAL INDIANA SENIOR FUND

Contents

Acknowledgments iii

Returning to the Lake: *Introduction with Suggestions for Writing Your Own Life Stories* v

Writing Assignments x

Jenny Allis 1
    The Milkman 2
    Revelation 3
    The Barn 5
    Eddie 5
    The Honor 7
    A Tradition 10

Claudia Britt 13
    Beginnings 14
    The Past in the Present 16
    The Wonder of Fall 18
    Quilts and Comforters—My Covers 20
    The Start of More to Come 22

Ward Britt 26
    My First Real Job 27
    Dad's Chaw of Tobacco 28
    Mealtime Grace 29
    Honor Platoon 30
    Staging Battalion 32
    "Bad Moon Rising" 34
    Divine Intervention 35
    Christmas Stockings 37

Patricia Clark 39
    Confessions of a Good Girl, or Vote, Vote for Miss Rheingold! 40
    The House on Washington Street 43

"Hello Darkness, My Old Friend"—December 1966,
  Orono, Maine   44
Groupe Scolaire Jean Butez   47
On the Train   49

Bill Culley   52
The Pony   53
Cousin Bob's Visit   55
The Untold Story   57
"When It's Springtime in the Rockies"   60
My New Life as a Dancer   61

Patricia Cupp   64
My War Years   65
Third Grade   68
Photographed Together on the Bridge He Built   71
Belonging to the Day: Remembering Ethiopia   72

Frisco Gilchrist   75
Frisco   76
Spanked or Not?   78
Earliest Memory   79
The Violin   80
Meeting Jedd   82

Beverly L. Harrington   85
The Red Slippers   86
The Fall of the Bully   87
Strangers in the Night   89

Linda Shaw   92
Barns   93
Going Back in Time   95
Hide and Seek   97
"Where the Boys Are"   100

About the Editor, Photographer and Cover Designer   105

Acknowledgments

The stories in *Returning* were written for the memoir class I taught in the autumn of 2011: "Everybody Has a Story: Write and Speak Yours." This project was supported by several non-profit organizations committed to the belief that our local community, as well as the larger human community, is richly served when seniors return to the past to tell us their stories.

Central Indiana Community Foundation (CICF) with a grant from the Central Indiana Senior Fund provided the project's financial support. Additional thanks go to the Writers' Center of Indiana, especially to Barb Shoup, Executive Director; Dr. Darolyn "Lyn" Jones, Summer Program Director, Memoir Project; and WCI's Board of Directors. The Indianapolis Senior Center provided us with a comfortable, centrally-located facility and Ben Lamey, Fine Arts and Technology Director for the Center, organized class scheduling and publicity.

I was also fortunate to have the assistance of WCI volunteers, Patricia Cupp and James Todd. They not only led small group discussions, but they also contributed their talents to *Returning*. Patricia helped me with editing and proofreading the text; James took photographs of class members.

Special thanks to Mark Latta for formatting this book and to Vienna Wagner for the cover photograph and design. Additional appreciation extends to others who graciously donated their time—to Iona Wagner who scanned and cropped the older photographs and to Chuck Wagner and Julianna Thibodeaux who gave me feedback on the introduction.

Finally, I want to thank the writers for their honesty and hard work. Their vividly-rendered stories reassure us that growing older does not mean our memory will fail us. They confirm what the poet Ted Kooser has said: ". . . how fortunate it is for all of us that the long-term memory is the most durable. We each have our country of memory always within us, always open to exploration, and we hold this for most of our lives."

Shari Wagner
Instructor
The Writers' Center of Indiana
www.indianawriters.org

Returning to the Lake
An Introduction with Suggestions for Writing Your Own Life Stories

I always enjoy going back to E.B. White's essay, "Once More to the Lake." Over the years I must have read it twenty or more times and still appreciate not only its evocative imagery and rhythms that mimic water but also its confluence of the past with the present and its setting: a lake in the woods where as a boy White and his family rented a cabin every August.

My family vacationed at such a lake, too. Actually, we fished and swam and sunned ourselves in a chain of lakes, each connected by a narrow channel edged by reeds and bullhead lilies. When I once again cross the sun-flecked waters of Oliver, Olin or Martin, it's as if I'm returning to my childhood. This is especially true on Olin, the lake with an undeveloped shoreline pictured on the cover of this book. As I gaze into the reflection of maples and tamaracks, the same trees our boat drifted over more than forty years ago, the passage of time seems an illusion; the past has a surface I can reach down to touch.

The stories in this book represent the journeys of nine remarkable people, none of them writers by trade, who go back to the past, to that deep, lucid reservoir of memory where nothing significant is lost. They find their way back by taking a road that might appear as only wheel tracks through overgrown grass. But this road brings us "once more to the lake" as one vividly rendered detail leads us to the next. "It is strange," White says in his essay, "how much you can remember about places like that [the lake] once you allow your mind to return into the grooves that lead back. You remember one thing, and that suddenly reminds you of another thing."

Allow is a key word. It's easy to set up self-imposed roadblocks before you even get started—to believe that you've forgotten too much or that your stories aren't important. In each of our class sessions, returning to the past began by reading aloud a passage by someone who had successfully skirted the barricades. I chose excerpts from works that modeled the specificity of sensory detail I wanted to see in each class member's stories and that suggested our next writing activity.

I know of no writing that depicts a setting more vividly than Eudora Welty's personal essay, "The Little Store." So for the first assignment, to describe a childhood place, we read aloud a portion of that reminiscence and then discussed how the store is recreated through sensual description (the smell of "dill-pickle brine that had leaked through a paper sack" and "the motes of cracker dust, cornmeal dust, the Gold Dust of the Gold Dust Twins"). We pointed out the rhythm of parallel phrasing and the comparisons that reflected a child's perspective—cheese "as big as a doll's house," for instance. We noted strong verbs ("hoisted," plunged," "fished out") and the pleasing repetition of vowels and consonants, such as the alliterative "s" in "the smell of still-untrapped mice." We admired how Welty could fuse sound and sense in a phrase like "the stiffest scissors."

Then we remembered places from our own childhood that offered strong sensory details: a three-room house smelling of six sweaty children, lilacs and soup or a barn so quiet you could hear cows flicking flies with their tails. One memory jogged another: the sharp scent of pine in a grandfather's workshop stirred forth memories of a kitchen where homemade sauerkraut permeated the air. For ten minutes, without pausing their pens, everyone jotted a list of all the sensory details they could recall relating to a childhood place. Spelling, penmanship and grammar had no bearing. Judgments of whether a detail was accurate or necessary we shoved aside for later. This was a way to find the "grooves that lead back," so that when class members actually began writing, each would have moved closer to the lake.

Supplementing this introduction is a list of all nine assignments, along with the guidelines and models I used and the titles of stories from *Returning* that exemplify each writing activity. The first assignments involve remembrances from childhood; later ones add the option of using memories from adolescence or adulthood. The writing activities also move from descriptive to narrative and then to assignments that offer more latitude in structure and sometimes use comparison or background information.

Beginning writers sometimes don't realize that published pieces such as "The Little Store" and "Once More to the Lake" represent the last stage of a process that began with disordered notes or a scruffy rough draft. The writer Anne Lamont describes the rough draft as "the child's draft, where you let it all pour out and then let it romp all over the place, knowing that no one is going to see it and that you can shape it later." That's the approach I tried to encourage as class members took home their first week's assignment. Going to the lake should be fun—a time to splash, to enjoy the fluidity of memory and the new insights that flash up from below.

Any writing becomes more pleasurable when it entails a sense of anticipation. That's why for the first assignment I told the class they didn't need to understand the significance of the childhood place before they began writing. They could discover its importance along the way. If you write from the mindset of setting down what you already know, you're more likely to become bored—and so will the reader. There won't be enough suspense to sustain your interest or lure you back to revise. But if you write from what you don't know—even when it pertains to your own memories—then curiosity will lure you back to each draft to see what new details or metaphors or epiphanies are pulling on the line.

While a portion of each class meeting was spent preparing for the next assignment, another part was devoted to listening and critiquing the previous week's work. When critiquing, we began with what we liked in a story, and there was *always* something to like—whether it was the subject matter, tone, insights or details. Then we discussed what might make the story better— sharper details, for instance, or information to provide context.

Not knowing how serious the class would be about revising their stories, I initially offered to write comments for just those writers who were interested. As it turned out, everyone was interested—for every assignment. Some writers even requested comments on subsequent revisions. I was impressed by the improvements I saw between drafts, the commitment to excellence you will sense as you read through this sampling of stories.

The fluidity so integral to memory and writing represents the same openness, the same flow of ideas from one lake to the next that I wanted us to experience in class. That's why I was delighted when students posed questions we could explore further, sometimes in a subsequent session. After one student asked, "Can you ever have too many details in a story?" we looked at chapter eight in Ted Kooser's book, *The Poetry Home Repair Manual.* What Kooser says in "Writing from Memory" is applicable to poetry and prose. He suggests allowing the rough draft to accumulate whatever details come to mind and then, in later drafts, carefully choosing between what's necessary and not. He compares this process of discernment to shopping the overcrowded tables at an estate sale. "Carry a little basket," he advises, ". . . and pick up only those details that you really want to use."

Sometimes class sessions were enhanced by works that members happened to read during the week and brought back to the group. "Dear Life: A Childhood Visitation" by Alice Munro (*The New Yorker*, September 19, 2011) connected beautifully with our assignment of writing about a childhood place. "Going Back," a poem by Gregory Djanikian, was an excellent model for assignment #5, revisiting a place.

When I recall summers at the lake, I think of the people who were with me. I remember how my sister, brother, parents and I, along with visiting cousins, aunts and uncles, would link floats as we relaxed upon the water. Afloat on our own inner tube or plastic raft, we held on to the string or corner of one or more other floats so that, in essence, our chain made a human knot that kept us near enough to share stories or to close our eyes without fear of drifting away.

Over the course of sharing stories once a week for eleven weeks, the writers in this book linked together as a community of writers. As we met in the home of one class member for a recent reunion brunch, I realized how close we had become and that I knew more about these people than I knew about neighbors with whom I'd been acquainted for ten years. I would advise anyone wishing to write their life stories to join a class or to form a writers' group. Such communities offer valuable feedback, discipline and friendship. Because the act of writing is such a solitary activity, it helps to be buoyed by others who affirm what you're doing.

Now, when my daughters and I dredge pearly mussels from the muddy edge of Oliver or form a tight knot on Olin with our floats, I have the sense that I'm returning to the past, living the same events over, but viewing them from the perspective of both a child and an adult. Such a return with its attendant insights is a gift we receive when we write from our memories. Patricia Hampl in *A Romantic Education* says, "To write about one's life is to live it twice, and the second living is both spiritual and historical, for a memoir reaches deep within the personality as it seeks its narrative form. . . ."

Carved by a glacier, Olin Lake is eighty feet deep at its center. But on its smooth, translucent surface the shadow of a boat slides over tamaracks. There's the soft dipping of wooden oars. The boat glides forward as we reach back.

Shari Wagner

Writing Assignments

Assignment #1: A Childhood Place
Describe a significant place from childhood that was rich with sensory details and memories. Include these details (of sight, sound, touch, smell or taste), at least three original comparisons (similes or metaphors), a beginning that draws in the reader and an ending that's memorable, that seems to ripple outward through an image or statement.

Model: "The Little Store" from *The Eye of the Story* by Eudora Welty
From *Returning*: "The Barn" by Jenny Allis; "Beginnings" by Claudia Britt; "The House on Washington Street" by Patricia Clark; "Earliest Memory" by Frisco Gilchrist; "The Fall of the Bully" by Beverly Harrington; "Barns" by Linda Shaw

Assignment #2: An Inheritance
Explain how a particular object from childhood connects you with a person or group of people. Include a vivid description of the object and person(s) involved. How does this object represent an inheritance of something you value?

Model: "Inheritance of Tools," from *The Paradise of Bombs* by Scott Russell Sanders
From *Returning*: "Quilts and Comforters" by Claudia Britt; "The Pony" by Bill Culley; "Photographed Together on the Bridge He Built" by Patricia Cupp; "The Violin" by Frisco Gilchrist

Assignment #3: Crossing the Line
Write about a time in your childhood or adolescence when you (or someone you knew) broke a rule, defied authority or acted against an expectation. As you tell your story, use sensory description and dialogue. Let the reader be privy to your thoughts. Use strong verbs and dramatize the point in the story where there is the most tension. Consider the consequences this situation had for you.

Model: Chapter 3 from *A Private History of Awe* by Scott Russell Sanders

From *Returning*: "The Milkman" by Jenny Allis; "Dad's Chaw of Tobacco" and "Staging Battalion" by Ward Britt; "Confessions of a Good Girl, or Vote, Vote for Miss Rheingold!" by Patricia Clark; "The Untold Story" by Bill Culley; "Third Grade" by Patricia Cupp; "Spanked or Not?" by Frisco Gilchrist; "The Red Slippers" by Beverly Harrington; "Hide And Seek" by Linda Shaw

Assignment #4: A Memory Associated with a Song

Share one or more memories that you associate with a song. If possible, listen to a recording before you write. Include some brief information about the song, one or more narratives when appropriate, vivid description and an exploration of why the song is important to you.

Another option: Instead of focusing on a song, explore the personal significance of a movie, book or painting.

Models: "Graduation" from *Innocence and Experience* by Maya Angelou and the poem, "I Ask My Mother to Sing" from *Rose* by Li-Young Lee

From *Returning*: "Bad Moon Rising" by Ward Britt; "Hello Darkness, My Old Friend—December 1966, Orono, Maine" by Patricia Clark; "When It's Springtime in the Rockies" by Bill Culley; "Where the Boys Are" by Linda Shaw

Assignment #5: Revisiting the Past

Reflect upon what it was like to revisit a certain place after the passage of many years. Include comparisons between past and present, descriptive details, strong verbs, dialogue if appropriate and what you learned from the experience.

Other options: Write about a time when another person took you along to visit a place from his or her past. What did you learn about this person through that visit? Or write about an event, such as a reunion or anniversary, which brought past and present together.

Model: "Once More to the Lake" from *Essays of E. B. White* by E.B. White
From *Returning*: "Revelation" by Jenny Allis; "The Past in the Present" by Claudia Britt; "Groupe Scolaire Jean Butez" by Patricia Clark; "Going Back in Time" by Linda Shaw

Assignment #6: A First Meeting
Tell a story about meeting someone for the first time. This initial encounter should be one that had important consequences for you. Make your story interesting through the use of setting, character description, action and dialogue. Think about gestures and facial expressions. Consider the effect that meeting this person had on your life.

Model: Chapter 13 from *A Private History of Awe* by Scott Russell Sanders
From *Returning*: "Eddie" by Jenny Allis; "The Start of More to Come" by Claudia Britt; "Divine Intervention" by Ward Britt; "My New Life as a Dancer" by Bill Culley; "My War Years" by Patricia Cupp; "Meeting Jedd" by Frisco Gilchrist; "Stranger in the Night" by Beverly Harrington

Assignment #7: Receiving (or Not Receiving) a Certain Distinction
Write about a distinction that you or someone close to you received or failed to receive. Consider why you wanted (or didn't want) this recognition or appointment. What did you do to try to get it (or not to get it)? What were the after-effects? Focus on details that will create suspense in your story. Use dialogue and gestures, along with descriptions of setting, character and action.

Model: "There She Is" from *A Girl Named Zippy: Growing Up Small in Mooreland, Indiana* by Haven Kimmell
From *Returning:* "The Honor" by Jenny Allis; "Honor Platoon" by Ward Britt; "On the Train" by Patricia Clark; "Frisco" by Frisco Gilchrist

Assignment #8: A Holiday Memory or Tradition
Focus on one memorable holiday. This holiday might be unforgettable for how much fun it was or for how things went horribly wrong. You might want to contrast this particular celebration with the usual tradition in your household, placing it in a context. Consider the significance of this holiday event and its consequences.
Another option is to describe a certain holiday tradition in your family. Choose one that's unique in some way. How did this tradition get started? Why have you kept it? (Or why have you discontinued it?) What threatens this tradition? How has it changed over the years? Use vivid details to describe this tradition and examples from particular years whenever relevant.

Models: Fifth chapter of "Citizenship in the Home" from *This Boy's Life* by Tobias Wolff and "A Christmas Memory" by Truman Capote
From *Returning*: "The Tradition" by Jenny Allis; "The Wonder of Fall" by Claudia Britt; "Mealtime Grace" and "Christmas Stockings" by Ward Britt; "Cousin Bob's Visit" by Bill Culley

Assignment #9: A Work-Related Memory
Write a story about one or more memories related to work. The work you focus on may be a childhood job or an adult profession, a favorite hobby or some special project you undertook. Use specific details and examples, strong verbs, dialogue and possibly some kind of interesting context—for example, how this work compared to other jobs you have held or to your initial expectations.

Models: "The Mason," from *Working* by Studs Terkel and Chapter 15 of *A Hundred Camels: A Mission Doctor's Sojourn and Murder Trial in Somalia* by Gerald L. Miller with Shari Miller Wagner
From *Returning*: "My First Real Job" by Ward Britt; "Belonging to the Day: Remembering Ethiopia" by Patricia Cupp

"The past is never dead. It's not even past."
William Faulkner, *Requiem for a Nun*

"We stared silently at the tips of our rods, at the dragonflies that came and went. I lowered the tip of mine into the water, tentatively, pensively dislodging the fly, which darted two feet away, poised, darted two feet back, and came to rest again a little farther up the rod. There had been no years between the ducking of this dragonfly and the other one—the one that was part of memory."
E. B. White, "Once More to the Lake"

Jenny Allis

Jenny was born in Detroit, Michigan but grew up in Central Lower Michigan, in a rural area, 12 miles from school, church and town.

After high school graduation, she attended Harper Hospital School of Nursing in Detroit and wrote her Boards in '64, a year after her marriage and shortly after the birth of her first child, a son. Her husband settled the family in Dayton, Ohio until he completed his commitment to the Air Force. While her husband studied for his PhD and worked at the University of Cincinnati, Jenny did part-time nursing and had a second child, a daughter, in '68.

In a series of job-related moves, the family eventually lived in Connecticut and California. Jenny began nursing for Hospice, becoming a member of a specialized AIDS Hospice team. She and her husband had three more children, another daughter and twin boys. One of the twins died in 1990.

Since 1999, Jenny and her husband have been living in Indianapolis where she has explored her interests in art, writing and traveling. Her children are married and live in Cincinnati with her "grandies."

The Milkman

We had a new little sister at our house. Though she was round and lovely, with curly hair, she was also fussy and demanding. I recall the time she became frustrated and started screaming, beating her spoon on the high-chair tray. Not obtaining the desired results, she began banging her head on the chair. This didn't continue long, only until the chair started to disintegrate, piece by piece.

We lived in a tiny house in a northwest Detroit suburb. My mom was of slight build and, as the sister of three big, teasing Irish brothers, who were rowdy and allowed to be so, she easily fell into feelings of being overwhelmed, even with her young children. One day, needing some respite from her cranky baby and inquisitive, creative three year old, she allowed her toddler to take her tricycle outside. It was a safe neighborhood, and limits had been established for distance of travel—"only to the corner," which was one house down the street. I was a "good girl" and a "pleaser." She thought she could trust me.

Out the door I went for a little "big girl" adventure. What could I do to make my freedom more fun? Try something new. Ah ha! The Twin Pines Dairy milkman had been to our front porch and delivered three quarts of milk in gleaming, glass bottles—their tall, fat necks covered with pleated paper caps that displayed stately green pines. I loved milk. It looked thick and creamy, and when chilled, it was delicious with cereal, sandwiches and, especially, cookies.

Since I couldn't wrestle the bottles in their protective metal crate onto my bike, I carefully loaded each bottle onto the nice, wide step behind my seat. This was going to be fun. I might really enjoy being a milkman. Off I rode, tooling around the corner just a little too fast. CRASH! One bottle was no more. Beautiful milk flowed on the sidewalk amid gleaming daggers and sparkling chips of shattered glass. I tried to turn around carefully, but—oops! There went bottle number two. Now what? Better get home fast and maybe Mom wouldn't notice. As I hurried up the slight incline of our driveway, number three met its end—and there was Mom.

Why don't I remember the outcome for me? Later, after a nap, I remember looking out the window. I saw no milk or glass and have no memory of being denied my favorite drink or any undue suffering.

I wish I could credit this experience as a life-changing moment. However, I remain terminally curious, though hopefully a little more responsible and, definitely, wiser in my choices.

Revelation

When I entered kindergarten, a new vista opened for me. Before that, my world consisted of my house, the one next door, the neighborhood store down the block, my Sunday school class and my grandparents' home, a 15 minute drive away. Then, when I was in first grade, another "window" opened when we went on our first family vacation.

Many people prefer not to eat fish. But I love fish, and I think the main reason is because our trip took us to Lake Huron, which was, at that time, with no expressways, a three-hour journey from Detroit. On the way, my dad bought freshly caught perch, lit a small stove at a roadside park and cooked our breakfast. The fish were delicious—tender and just about the best thing I'd ever eaten. Later we swam in a lake where we couldn't even see the other side. For a long way from shore, the water stayed shallow and my sister and I played with our favorite kewpie doll, the one with a squeaker. We had so much fun that we couldn't find Squeaker when it was time to go, so I guess she played there forever.

Then we crossed the Blue Water Bridge into Canada. It's at the bottom of Lake Huron, where it flows into the St. Clair River that runs between Michigan and Ontario. The bridge was huge, and the water shone amazing shades of blue. When we got off, we drove into the country, to the tiny town of Dresden.

Outside of town, not very far, was my father's favorite boyhood place—his cousin Horace's farm. Horace lived in a tall, thin red brick house on a flat piece of land with few trees. It seemed large and handsome. There were several barns, an old tractor and a pair of work horses.

Inside the home, the large rooms were filled with heavy furniture. The round table served grand meals with many selections, including beef and ham, corn, beans, yams, fluffy potatoes, pickles, pickled beets, applesauce, white and brown bread with homemade strawberry jam and for dessert, either apple or rhubarb pie. The table was set with the Sunday best, and we were given paper napkins, as at home, but here they were called "serviettes." We were expected to be on our best behavior, and I recall no "incidents."

Behind the barn and down a steep slope with a road, there was a stream of slow moving water. To reach the fields on the other side, this stream had to be forded. Driving down to the water and through it seemed strange and fascinating to a city girl who was told not to play in the water around her home. I could see why my dad loved this farm and these people I'd never met before.

A few years later, when we moved to a farm 60 miles west of Detroit, I wasn't surprised to see my dad reliving his childhood in a rural area that I also came to love. He raised sheep, pigs, chickens, horses, rabbits and dogs while he continued a factory job. We could only see one neighbor's house and that was about a fourth of a mile away. After the road passed our house, grass grew down the middle of it.

My city-girl mom was never totally comfortable there, but her daughter was a convert. Though I left the farm after high school graduation and married a man whose work dictated city life, I still dream of living once more in the beauty and open space of the country.

The Barn

The Michigan farm of my growing up years had a wonderful barn. Winter or summer, it welcomed me. At one time it was painted silver, and the remaining paint and aging boards gave it a buffed glow. The foundation stones supported wide boards with slight cracks spaced between them. Rays of sunlight crept through the walls, with chaff and dust motes floating in the stream.

The barn offered shelter from the hot sun and protection from the cold. Swirling snowflakes built small drifts on the floor and hay. Straw and chaff gave the floor a slight slipperiness. Feral cats slunk in and out, dodging from our attention but never far away, always hoping for a discarded morsel.

An old tractor, a sharpening wheel and other farm equipment littered one side of the floor. The other half of the large front area was filled with bales of hay and bedding straw. These bales offered exciting places to hide and burrow and made ideal building blocks for forts.

Though rickety in appearance, the barn was supported by 8 x 8 inch square beams that only the most daring child would walk across, 16 or so feet above the floor. My bravery did not extend to such physical feats.

Behind the hay, in the back, were three stalls and a small area for cows and horses. Outside was a fenced in barnyard where our horses exercised and sheep huddled when not grazing in the pasture. In the spring we loved to watch the lambs as they skipped and vaulted.

Eddie

Though I lived 12 miles away from the town where I went to school and church, the town kids were my friends, the people I grew up with. Two of the girls, Lois and Ruth, were my special friends and still are, though we live states apart. The boys in the group were a little older and were never our "boyfriends." The dynamic trio, Glen, Dick and Eddie, fit nicely in the category of "PEST."

After my high school graduation, Dick wanted to ask Lois out but thought he would have a better chance if his friend Eddie asked me and we doubled up. His idea worked. It was the Fourth of July weekend, just after graduation, and I'd had dates with others but decided to close out the holiday playing miniature golf with my three friends. To my way of thinking, Eddie led the pack in "pestiness," always teasing and pulling pranks. Eddie had written to me once during his junior year at Michigan State University, and I thought he was starting to grow up, but I never got around to responding. For this date, I was just going along for the ride.

Lois went home first and never dated Dick again. Ed and I had a long ride to my home, and we had a very nice conversation. Even when we'd arrived, we sat talking longer. We did a lot of "getting acquainted chat," discussing likes and dislikes, places we'd like to go and some hopes and dreams. We were clicking! I was surprised that he could be so nice. And yes, there was a kiss—not something usual for either of us.

The next morning, my family asked me about the date. Surprising, even to me, were my words to my mom: "I think I'll marry him."

Her response was, "Oh, no, not Eddie." Mom spent many years teaching Sunday school, and when she realized the next group of students would be the "Terrible Trio," she resigned. It's been years since she's passed on, but my husband says she went "out the door" saying it and continues still . . . "Oh, no, not Eddie." (Would you be surprised to hear that I've never called him Eddie?)

Maybe my mom's words should have held more weight than I gave them, for marriage to Ed has not been easy. . . sometimes even hard. Our Meyers-Briggs test shows he has the personality of a commandant and I, one like Joan of Arc, a lady of strong ideas and leadership abilities. Major conflict is inevitable. But he is a great provider, smart, fun, faithful, generous and pretty kind—though he is still a tease. His personal test to see if he's alive each day is to do a "gotcha" on me. After nearly 49 years of marriage, peace has come and we enjoy each other, agreeing on most things and laughing a lot. Our special bonus is our five wonderful children, their spouses and our "grandies" . . . nine so far.

The Honor

By the time Ed and I had been married 15 years, we had a daughter, age 10 and a son, 14. As a child, I had dreamed of more children, but because of a rocky relationship and some feelings of failure as a parent, I'd given up that idea. These things considered, my husband and I began to discuss sterilization. It seemed to me a simple thing for my husband to do. It didn't happen. No problem, I'd do it. But then, into my busy mind came a pause . . . whoa . . . hold up. I was considering a profound decision. We needed divine guidance. Ed and I prayed and gave God a six month window to give us a child or we would move on. Vacationing in Arizona, climbing up from the depths of the Grand Canyon with the energy of a slug, I knew after eleven years that I was pregnant again, and I was more than delighted.

The next spring we were given a joyful, social little girl who loved her teenage sibs and their friends. She cried little and her deep eyes added much to the image of an "old soul." As she neared two years old, Ed and I thought that we should ask for divine wisdom on the question of whether it would be best for Peggy to grow up essentially alone or if she needed a sibling. Due to the circumstances of moving and of not wanting too large of a gap between children, there was no three month window this time. It was this month or never.

We were in the midst of moving from Connecticut to a small town in Northern Ohio. The ten hour drive in two cars, with three kids, including a toddler who didn't travel well and a teenager doing some of the driving on his new permit, created a bit of a hair-raising trip, to say the least. Arriving at the town I privately dubbed "End of the Road," we were escorted to a suite in the town's only hotel. How sweet is a double bed, two daybeds and a port-a-crib squished into a small room? Exhausted, we ate our pizza dinner there and the teens crashed on the daybeds and were sleeping soundly in moments. Baby slept, too. As Ed and I were turning in, though, she awakened and vomited all over her crib. We cleaned her up and put her in our bed, just a little too soon. . . She baptized our bed, too. Room service, new linens, clean baby—at last we could turn in. Peace was descending. Silently, my husband started caressing me. Roused, I asked, "What are you doing?" No answer.

    A few weeks after moving to Ohio, I knew I was pregnant. Six or eight weeks later, in my new "Doc's" office, I read an article on multiple births as I waited. It stated that multiple births were often achieved when women were over 35 and had very regular, short cycles. Doc asked how I was, and I replied, "Nervous," citing my new information. His response was not to comment.

    This was my fourth pregnancy and though all of the pregnancies were slightly different, this one was markedly so. The baby seemed very active very early. I thought I was having a "Downs syndrome" child. I also figured if this was so, God knew and had sent this one to us and I'd better 'saddle up' and make it all right with me. Time passed and I had a sonogram. I saw two babies. Deep in denial, I reasoned that there were two pictures of one baby, of course. Three weeks later, returning from my father-in-law's funeral, I received a call from Doc. It started, "Are you sitting down?" Was he kidding me? I was huge, I loved sitting down these days! "You're having twins."

    I was speechless—a miracle for a "Chatty-Cathy" girl like me. My 16 year old son came by and said, "What?"

    I mumbled, "Twins." And he was the one who broke the news to his father. A new town, a new house, a new church, a new Doc, a new hairdresser, and an 'old' mother (age 39) with no old friends near and a two year old. For all this, I had no comment.

Two days before I was due, as I was cutting drapes for my living room, a new friend dropped by. "What are you doing?" she asked.

"Cutting drapes," I replied.

"What are you writing down?"

"Nothing, just a few little practice twinges I'm feeling."

"I'm calling Doc."

"No." But she called anyway and Doc said to go the hospital. He'd come in when the office closed at five. It was 2 pm. After an uneventful admission, I figured I'd need my strength for labor, so I decided to take a nap. It was a nice sleep. Around five, I thought maybe I'd better stroll the ward a little and get things moving. I heard a "pop" and felt a gush. My water had broken. Within the next hour, my husband had arrived and we had two new sons who weighed seven pounds each.

I was the mother of twins. I learned later that I shouldn't have been surprised, as both my maternal grandparents had twin siblings.

Due to my age, my toddler and the resulting lack of energy, I observed these boys much more than I had my other children. These two little guys were so equally endowed, so alike and yet so different. I was fascinated. Our teenagers, having already experienced a baby in the family, were making themselves scarce. My toddler, casting aside the doll we'd brought for her when we came home with the boys, became a great help as it was clear she had decided there was, "One baby for Mom and one baby for me."

Babyhood was busy but fine. Toddlerhood with the little ones was twice as interesting and stimulating for them and me. Jim and Drew really liked each other and their little sis but could so easily, without a word, initiate some "dastardly deeds." For example: adding dirt in the lawnmower's gas tank, flushing pencils that got stuck in the toilet, throwing various and sundry things down the laundry chute, and more deeds came as they grew older and we moved four more times. But I loved being the mother of twins, despite the extra work. It was unsought, but an honor, truly an amazing gift from God. I felt so blessed.

Since we held Jim and Drew back from kindergarten, they were eight, almost nine, when they started into second grade. Labor Day weekend, Drew, our first-born, was sick with the flu. We went to the doctor. His temperature soared, and we returned to the E.R. Our son was admitted and just as the doctor showed up, he arrested. Eighteen days, three operations and many life-support machines later, Drew went to be with the Jesus he had learned to love during his short life.

I can't express how terribly sad it is to have a child pass. Thinking, mulling, cogitating, remembering, regretting, ruing, I moved through the mourning process. I know Drew is safe and happy and whole and with Jesus who loves him totally and with grandparents who dote on him. But our loss is grievous for us and especially for his twin brother, Jim. And I bear the private grief of no longer feeling or believing I am the mother of twins.

It's been 21 years now and as time passes, I grow to know that Drew is really alive and more than well. He is happy and healthy and tremendously loved and appreciated. My conviction is that his life is wonderful. I'm so persuaded I no longer think of him in that graveyard in Ohio and never care to visit there anymore.

Recently, we lit a lantern that floated upward, into a velvet black, moonless sky. It was inscribed with messages of yearning, love and anticipation of happy reunion. What a grand celebration we will some day have.

A Tradition

Each December my kitchen fills with the smell of gingerbread and the sounds of pandemonium:

"I want the red sparkles."
"No, that's my color."
"I don't have enough shingles for my roof."

"Send the silver balls my way."
"Where's the frosting bag?"
"No. I need the one with the little tip."
"Mine."
"Oh, Santa fell over!"
"I need more green jellybeans for my fence."
"Bussy, no. Stop eating all the candy."
"Here, Lyddy, let Mama help you."

Would you believe I brought all this chaos on myself? A typical project, plus Jenny, adds up to exponential growth and craziness.

About 20 years ago I bought a gingerbread house mold at a Longaberger Basket party. The mold, the process and the recipes were intriguing, the accompanying pictures enchanting. My junior high daughter, Peg, and grade school son, Jim, and I were going to make gingerbread houses. Laborious work involving a lot of tricks we failed to completely master got us to the decorating stage. "Enchanting" houses were a result we've never quite accomplished. But, oh, such joy as we created a long lasting treat that smelled so good. . . Of course, we had to eat every crumb. In such an innocent and pleasurable way, our Christmas tradition began.

Peg's older sister, Sue, married and had a son, Tim. Her brother, Jon, married and had a daughter, Jenn. Well, didn't these toddlers need to have houses to decorate? In only a few years, both "grandies" had sister siblings, Jessie and Mary. Then there were Sara and Andrew, two more for Jon. It wasn't long until Peg married and had Peter who was eager to join the crew. His daddy had a lot of fun helping him. . . . Hey, wasn't it his idea to have the dog peeing on the bush next to the gingerbread house? Next came Pete's twin sisters, Lydia and Elizabeth, dubbed "Bussy" by her cousin, Valery.

Is this tradition out of control? Yes, but how can we stop? My kids are the kind that only marriage gives their mother a pass on Easter Baskets. On the hopeful side, I already have a grandie who helps me build the houses, a pre-decoration operation.

Look out kids, Grammie's looking for a baker. But don't worry; I'll give you lots of practice. We need three batches of gingerbread to make houses for the nine of you.

Claudia Britt

Claudia grew up in a small town near the place of her birth in Central Indiana during the first wave of baby boomers. By the age of 20, she was employed as a registered nurse and worked in that field until her retirement.

Her joys in life have focused on her husband, three children and church activities. Early hobbies included sewing and reading. Later interests involved dancing, photography and genealogy. Then in 2002, she discovered a love for writing and joined two informal writing groups.

She loves to travel and hopes to find time to develop her interest in painting. In her spare time, she works Sudoku puzzles and is trying to learn Spanish. She continues to reside in her home state with her family, two Great Danes and a cat.

Beginnings

As I clutched Raggedy Ann tightly in my arms, Dad carried me up the short sidewalk to our first little house. Though it was just a rental, it was all ours with more space and privacy than were available in the three other places we had lived. It was a lovely white cottage framed by leafy trees and lilac bushes.

Upon crossing the wooden front porch, we entered the house through the front door. I could see straight through to the back porch door and beyond. Mom and Dad's bedroom was at the right front. There was no closet, but a curtain, hung over a strung wire, sectioned off a corner for hanging clothes. Behind the bedroom was the kitchen. Space was cramped by the table, chairs, Sellers Cabinet (a wood and porcelain kitchen cabinet made from the turn of the 20th century into the depression era), refrigerator, stove and sink. The living room on the left ran the length of those two rooms. Strips of flowers ran up and down the wallpaper, and the slate-blue drapes had scattered blossoms, large and white. The bathroom, with its tub and sink, was behind the kitchen and next to the enclosed back porch.

Our cozy little three-room cottage started out with three occupants: Mom, Dad and me. Six years later, our family of three had grown to eight—three girls, three boys and two parents. We were "stair-step" children—small, smaller and smallest—all under six years old. This was the beginning . . . the start of it all in my memory.

The back porch became a bunk room for us, the four oldest children. Dad built bunk beds using scrap lumber. Though we were poor, we children didn't know it. Custom built beds were a great adventure for us. We girls were on the south end of the porch, and the boys were on the north. Two full-size cribs stood end to end in the living room, on the opposite side of the wall from the boys' bunks. My top bunk was built from an old wooden ironing board. Back then, ironing boards were wider than the metal ones are today. It was special to me and just the right size. I rested well, with my tattered quilt and a thick, dark, scratchy wool comforter for the winter. At last, my parents had a room of their own, free of a crib.

Plenty of crying, laughing, arguing and talking filled the air, along with, of course, the voice of the trusty old radio. No such thing as a TV or telephone existed in our small world. Verbal communication involved a face to face encounter by running out the back door and across the yard to Grandmother's house at the end of the block. Mother could write letters to family or friends, if she found the time.

The smells we encountered came from sweaty bodies, mud pies and hearty soups; from heating oil in winter and vases of lilacs or zinnias in summer. Mother loved fresh flowers for scenting the house. Green beans and other vegetables harvested from the garden, as well as peaches from the farmers' market, filled the air with warm aromas as they were canned for winter. Mom and Grandma made sauerkraut in a large, round brown crock, with a plate covering the top.

We learned to love the taste of lime Kool-Aid, crisp rhubarb, firm red grapes, soft yellow peaches and crusty chocolate batter pudding. Ice cream and popcorn were special treats for Sundays. My sister ate mud pies, but I don't recall if she really liked them or if they were an experiment. She ended up covered all over with caked mud.

Summer was more fun than winter because we all escaped to the great outdoors. The hardened mud path between our house and the next was narrow but allowed our train of tricycles, Taylor Tots (a 1930-40s era stroller/walker), wagons and bare feet just enough room to travel back and forth from front to backyard, over and over. Grass grew thick in back but sparse in front. My little sister made her mud pies in the front yard; then she would swing contentedly on the porch, wearing only her diaper and splotches of leftover mud.

We could run and play and be loud outside. It was a joyful release from the restraint of being relatively quiet inside the house. We girls wore "gold" canning ring bracelets from wrist to elbow and felt ever so lovely until

Mother reclaimed them for the canning of green beans and peaches.

In the house, six little red rocking chairs sat in a semi-circle around the living room stove on the side wall. I see them as they were at Christmas time. On Christmas morning, we would each find a gift on our chair. I remember my big brown teddy bear greeting me there as he completely filled the small seat. He was just my size and a faithful companion for many years.

When our family was complete, we outgrew our cozy cottage. "Snug" turned into "pressed together." We needed breathing room. Our beds seemed to grow shorter as we grew longer. The time came to say, "Goodbye little house; we've got to go. But we'll take you along in our memories. Thanks for all the good ones."

The Past in the Present

Strangely enough, familiar places from my past often seem like strangers to me. I have the right address, but can this really be right? It's so small. There is no way a little white cottage, housing eight people, and a one-story duplex, housing five people on one side and two on the other, could fit on that empty lot. And Grandmother's brown shingled house has shrunk as well. The sidewalk to the front street is so short. There's barely room for the porch swing to the left of the screen door. What scientific process of decline has possessed this place to reduce it to this small plot of land?

The backyard used to be divided into a large garden space for the cottage and play area for the children, a smaller garden for the duplex, and a shed for tools attached to the long, low building that housed the rabbit cages behind Gram's house. The grape arbor was in back of Gram's house to the east, and there was space on the south side for the curtain stretchers she used annually for drying the laundered lace that covered her windows.

We children were usually confined to our own backyard; though no fences were in evidence, everyone knew the boundaries. I remember being so bold as to run across the long backyard to Gram's house all by myself when I was in kindergarten. I remember the pleasure. It was wonderful and freeing to "fly" over that great distance on sweet spring breezes as fast as my little four-year-old legs could carry me. I was quite pleased with myself. Mother was not so excited about my excursion. She said I was bare and scolded me severely for going out in my dress without my underwear.

Mr. Moon and his wife lived catty-cornered from Gram in a white two-story house that was much larger than Gram's house. About two blocks away was the corner grocery store that Mr. Moon owned. His store was the first floor of a house directly across the street from Marian College. It always seemed very spacious when my siblings and I walked over to get a soup bone for Gram. While we were there, he might give us some overly ripe bananas for bread or mini loaves of soft white bread for our very own use. Now I see that the store was just a regular house, and I can't imagine how he was able to arrange it with all the necessities. Mr. Moon wore a white shop apron which sometimes showed evidence of his butchering activities for the meat counter in the back. There were canned goods, cleaning agents and fresh produce on separate aisles. Though the quantities and variety of brands could not compare with today's supermarkets, they were sufficient for the college students and local neighborhood folks.

I always feel a little sad when I return to places of past influence. Why? Perhaps just because they are past, gone from my grasp. What memories are buried so deeply that I'll never find them? What part did this place play in developing me into the person I am today? Have I lost any part of myself there that I'd like to reclaim? My perspective has changed, and I can look back with adult eyes enlightened by the relentless marching on of time. Life's journey reshapes my views. Perhaps I need to find some healing there.

In some places, time seems to stand still. The view from our summer home on Little Chapman Lake is like this. There is no change. The sun rises and sets precisely as it has ever since I was a teenager. The breeze gently caresses my ears after it passes through the large leafy maples at the back of the property next to the channel. The rhythmic waves bouncing off the seawall lull me into complacency. There is no rush to go, to be, to do, to see, to experience more and more and more. There is just the quiet presence of the here and now. Calm, soothing ambiance. I am surrounded by it and never want to leave. I savor the subtle promise that all will be well, somehow, some way.

I love to return to the lake and spend quiet hours idling away the day in pleasant contemplation and reminiscence of old memories. I hug them to me tightly so that nothing can take them away. Why do I revisit past places? Perhaps it's a gift I am giving myself, a heart-felt celebration that nourishes my soul as I recall all the people and settings that have made me into the person I have become.

The Wonder of Fall

October arrives with its chilly evenings and darkness that creeps backward, up the clock to shorten the days. The leaves boldly color the landscape but fade quickly to blanket the grass in crisp layers, overflowing onto the sidewalks. Though allergies descend with falling leaves, the threat of sniffles is not great enough to hamper autumn celebrations. I am reminded of scuffing through the crackling leaves of Halloweens long past, stirring up dry dust and wet mold.

In October, the smell of heat pervades the house, burning off summer's dust, while outside the fragrance of burning leaves lingers to scent the air and seep inside. But some leaf piles are just for jumping in. Our grade school yard had an abundance of fallen leaves which the boys and tomboys gathered into a huge mountain. Running and shouting with glee, they jumped into the peak, scattering leaves to every side. We more domestic girls arranged leaves into discrete rows to outline the rooms of a house we played in. Of course, throwing leaves toward the sky created a lovely way to shower! Having no technological games to distract us, we kept well-connected with nature. These outside activities burned restless grade school energy, yet it was difficult to sit contentedly in class while the beautiful autumn awaited us on the playground. With winter on the way, we had to make the most of the time that was left.

Our town of about a thousand was a safe place where kids in the city limits walked to school and participated in school events even after dark, in summer and winter. I enjoyed the quiet atmosphere and felt secure in this place where everyone knew everyone else.

Trick or treat night was a big event for us. We mostly stayed in our own end of town, going door to door in our costumes. The goal, of course, was to get as much candy as we could. Candy was scarce at our home. We could only expect it on Christmas, Easter and Halloween. We knew what would be offered at each house we visited. Our neighbor, Mrs. B., always made popcorn balls. There were candy bars, apples, homemade cookies and taffy along our route. One old curmudgeon gave us hot banana peppers, fresh from his garden, to discourage a return the following year. It worked, too.

The whole town was invited to the Halloween party at the Conservation Club. This was the one time each year that we entered the building since we were not members, though, as Brownies and Girl Scouts, we were permitted to walk the grounds collecting leaves, acorns and walnuts.

At the party, there was always a line to bob for apples floating in the galvanized wash tubs. The crowd's noisy good humor echoed from the low-roofed rafters. Candy, cider and a costume contest were part of the fun. Prizes were given, based on age and such categories as: scariest, most beautiful, most original and hardest to guess. All those in costumes paraded around the interior in a circle while the judges looked on. The room seemed huge and very long as we slowly made our way around. No one had a formal costume—all involved makeshift ingenuity. There were cowboys, pirates, clowns, ghosts, witches, scarecrows, princesses, hoboes, Raggedy Anns, and others. Though I dressed up, I never won and was always identified early in the contest. My beanpole figure and smile below my half-mask always gave me away.

Win or lose, it's still fun to pretend. Some of my favorite pictures are of my children dressed as clowns or medical doctors, complete with mustaches before a stroll through the neighborhood on Halloween. I even have a red and turquoise clown suit with a frilly collar for myself, but I can't find my purple hair! So I content myself with gazing at the colorful leaves before they leave the trees. Watching them fall, I mourn their loss and bury them in a bag as I await the new generation in the spring that promises another glorious, though brief autumn.

Quilts and Comforters—My Covers

Oh crazy quilt of brightly-colored printed fabrics,
you are covered with fine smooth cottons
cut into angular shapes;
connected by many tiny stitches of thread;
precisely matched along lines and corners;
fashioned into a work of art;
yet you are so practical and functional. . . .;
appropriate for my daily use.

Hours of careful planning preceded your birth;
many nights of candlelight flickered
before your form was revealed
in neatly connected fabric squares of reds and yellows.
Your loving warmth enfolds me gently,
earning you a place as priceless
treasure of the fortunate possessor.
And that would be me.

My childhood quilt had many colors, but one stands out. It was a fragile and frayed pale yellow scrap near the top edge. The pattern involved circles of some kind, perhaps a Dresden plate or flower garden. The quilt was lightweight as the three sandwiched layers are meant to be—heavier than a sheet but lighter than a winter comforter. The backing was worn icy smooth, cool as window glass and was deliciously soothing to my skin. Weight is so important. I cannot sleep well without this proper weight even now in our modern age with such a huge variety of coverings to choose from. I was trained by the restful hours beneath my quilt to expect a certain weight signifying well-being and security. There is such comfort in the even pressure of the coverings.

As I think myself back into the distant past, the past is now present and I see and hear….squishy little sounds almost unnoticeable as I turn from side to side, taking the covers with me. The covering is so flexible, that I can roll up in it like a mummy, letting no heat escape from the long, narrow lump lying on top of the bed. I can cover my head to block out the light from the street, hold in the heat and smell the sweet warm air of my own breath. I am alive and present with myself. It is enough.

The quilts in our house are hand-me-downs as most of our things are. They connect me to my forbears who engaged in the long detailed process of quilt-making. Perhaps they belonged to Grandma, Great-Grandma or a great-aunt. I know Mother had no time to stitch up a quilt, though she did weave a baby blanket for me, the firstborn of six children in as many years. The blanket is blue and creamy white, fitting for a boy. My parents were hoping for a boy and thus named me after my grandfather, Claude.

The quilt fabrics represent dresses, aprons and shirts our family members have worn. Old or new, the pieces were recycled into a useable form. Nothing was wasted. Connections. . .belonging . . .desirability. . . the quilt speaks of these.

My comforter is much the same, except it is heavier. The back is flannel, the middle is cotton batting or a sheet blanket if one could be found; the front is made of rectangles, cut into 5x5 inch pieces from dark shades of scratchy wool. The wool pieces were stitched together on a machine; then the three layers were knotted together with red yarn to keep them from shifting. I am grateful for the comforter's warmth but hate that irritating textured wool to touch my skin. I keep my arms safely under the covers where the flannel backing is soft and reassuring. When the cold is unbearable, with ice on the windows and in the water cup, and the wind howls, echoing from one end of the room to the other, more than one comforter is needed. The weight is so great, that I can barely turn over beneath the pile stacked on the bed!

My memories over the past 64 years inspired me to attempt making some quilts for myself. The nicest was a sampler of five patterns which I machine pieced for a class at the Indianapolis Senior Center in 2007 or 2008. It took about three months to hand quilt the full-size covering for our bed. I have made only two stitched quilts in my entire life. The other one was of hexagon-shaped flowers which I began to hand stitch as I talked to my husband on the phone during our courting days. For each of our three children, I have made tie down comforters with flannel backings and a child-size cotton tie down bedspread for our young daughter to match her pink bunny curtains.

Quilts and comforters bring security by their warmth, weight and color. They say that someone cares and has invested their energy to create lovely, useful coverings. I guess that's how comforters got their name. Strength and renewal seep through as they shelter me.

The Start of More to Come

The Friday night gatherings of our Intervarsity Christian Fellowship Group were well attended by those in the college community of Indianapolis for their fun, friendship, food and nationally known speakers. I was a recent grad from the three year diploma nursing program at Wishard. My roommates and I were still of the proper age to continue attending these meetings which were hosted at my home church during the school year. The meeting format remained the same all year round though in winter our activities were all contained inside the church basement. The round robin table tennis games became quite competitive and challenging with the large number of players crowded around and the quick reflexes required to remain in the game to the end.

During the summer, there was a heavier emphasis on outdoor fun and games, which the lengthening daylight allowed. We played volleyball and croquet on the lawn. At dusk, we all entered the roomy basement of Dr. Smith's house and listened intently to our speaker. Discussion, questions and fellowship followed over cookies and lemonade. Sometimes, after we were talked out, we went out to eat at the Tee Pee, a popular drive-in on 38th Street.

This year the party to mark the end of the old semester and beginning of the new was held at the home of my former boyfriend. As usual, many kids attended. Although I knew a good number of the other students, every week there were strangers to meet and befriend. It was an exciting social season. Even now, 40 + years later, I am thrilled to run into long lost friends from those years. We catch up on our marriages, children, health, church attendance and whatever we can in the few minutes stolen from our assigned errands.

On June 1, 1972, the weather was co-operative with sunshine and pleasant temperatures throughout the evening. The party set-up afforded plenty of opportunities to mingle. The in-ground swimming pool was open, and there was a billiards table located in the garage, volleyball out on the grass, croquet wickets at the back of the property and tables for snacks and chats.

As usual, I played volleyball—on this occasion wearing my bright yellow knit shirt and dark brown polyester, slim-cut bell bottom slacks. The guys playing were always very aggressive and "chivalrous," smacking the ball when it looked like I was not going to be there in time. But now and then, I got it over the net with great success. I could serve pretty well when it was my turn. There was a new young man standing near me so we met and talked sporadically between plays. Then he, Ward, sat next to me when we watched a silent movie in the semi-darkness. Later, I saw him playing pool with a friend of mine in the garage. Apparently, Jim and Ward knew each other from the past. And too soon the evening was over.

The next Friday, I attended the meeting as planned. Surprisingly, this new guy returned. He knew only a few people there, so we talked the usual chitchat required to become better acquainted. As the weeks went on, he continued to come. At some point, Ward asked me out. At some point, I said, "Yes." Our first dates did not go well, but that is another story altogether. We spent long hours talking on the telephone, and he sent me beautiful red roses frequently. Love blossomed gently, and we became engaged in November of 1972.

Interestingly, my friend Lonnie told me that I had met Ward before the party. Ward had been with him when he came over to the nursing school to provide transportation for my friend Amy and me. We were going to the Jerome Heinz Opera at Clowes Hall. It was a Christian opera in the mid-1960s and a very special event for us to attend. Lonnie explained that Ward was helping with the opera since he attended a sponsoring church. At first I did not recall meeting him; but gradually, I retrieved the vague memory of a scrawny teenager sitting in the backseat as we took our places in the car. Perhaps I even sat next to him. He seemed so young. In 1966, I was 19, so Ward was only 16. He was a high-schooler, and I was a mature college student! Thus I did not pay much attention to him.

Isn't life strange? Truly timing is everything. Readiness to perceive can't be rushed. When I met Ward the first time, I perceived him as a mere child. And I was a student focused on learning a trade in order to support myself. I felt really grown up and way ahead of him in life. I learned later that Ward was advanced far beyond me in his experiences of life. He had more street smarts at 16 than I will ever have or need—since I have him. After his experiences in the Marine Corps, he had been exposed to more situations requiring maturity than I could ever know. His life at 22 was jam-packed full of rich life experiences with all their negative and positive challenges.

And now you can see that June 1, 1972, will always be a red letter day for me. I had left the apartment, blithely, not suspecting that the evening would have any lasting impact. It was the "last day of winter." It was the "first day of summer." It became the first day of a new direction that affected the rest of my life.

Ward and I married in April of 1973, ten months after our fateful meeting. The adventures continue, one day at a time.

Ward Britt

Ward is married, has three grown children and currently lives in Indianapolis.

He completed a BS in Marketing from Indiana University in 1977 using the GI Bill and a BS in Computer Technology in 2006. Additionally, he earned two certificates in web design and completed the A+ and Network+ certifications.

He has worked as a purchasing agent, a manufacturer's representative for wholesalers of hardware industry items and has managed a department of a wholesale hardware firm and retail chain stores.

Ward was appointed a Kentucky Colonel for service to country and volunteer work for disabled and homeless veterans. He is a service-connected disabled veteran due to toxic exposure and other combat related issues while serving in Vietnam. He is also a lifetime member of the Disabled American Veterans organization and the Marine Corps League.

My First Real Job

It seems like I have always worked. At age eight I started selling an early edition of the *Indianapolis News, The Blue Streak,* after school behind the downtown Sears store. In the summer I always had yards to mow, bushes to trim, weeds to pull, even vegetables to pick, and in the winter, I shoveled snow. But my first real job, at age fifteen, was at Standard Grocery at the Glendale Mall where my older brother was already working as a stock boy. I wanted to do what he was doing—pricing boxed and canned goods, stocking shelves and straightening merchandise on display.

The store manager had another idea and stuck me in the produce section. I hated it. I didn't like trimming cauliflower (especially after I sliced my thumb) or removing rotten potatoes, apples, oranges and various other fruit and vegetables from bags. Cleaning up the dead leaves that fell off or pulling the ones off that were near dead was too much like the yard work I had grown to hate. Over the weeks I repeatedly asked the store manager if he would move me to stock work, only to see him hire someone new for the stock department when an opening did become available. I developed an attitude of, "If I'm in produce then that's the only work I'll do."

One Saturday morning a customer asked me where the butter was. I told him it was in the butter case and pointed him in that direction. He said there was no butter there and asked if I could check in the cooler. Grudgingly, I went to the back room and looked in the cooler which was filled, wall-to-wall, with metal crates of milk. They were stacked about four feet high, but I could see that the shelves where the butter was supposed to be, back behind all that milk, were empty. I told the customer we evidently were out of butter because the shelves were empty.

Turns out, this guy was a friend of the store manager and he naturally went to him to complain about the lack of butter in the store. The manager came to me and said there was plenty of butter back there in the cooler. I responded that I had looked and the shelves were empty. He crooked his finger at me, said, "Come with me," and led me back to the cooler. When he flung open the door, he discovered what I already knew, the shelves were empty. He said, "Well, the butter is on the floor behind the milk," like I was somehow supposed to know that.

When he said, "Get it out," I reached for the crate of milk on top of the nearest stack to make a path back to the alleged butter. He rudely shoved me out of the way and said, "That's not the way to move the milk." He then reached up inside the cooler, over the door and pulled down a hidden, long hooked metal gadget for grabbing the bottom crate to slide the whole stack out of the way. In his zeal to instruct me in this fine art, he tipped the top crate so that a gallon of milk fell and burst on the floor, covering his shiny black shoes with creamy white liquid. At the same time, another carton of milk in that tilted top crate split open and poured down the front of his dress trousers. I couldn't help myself and had to laugh at his misfortune.

He stormed angrily away, only to return about an hour later, after I had dutifully stocked the butter case full of new one pound packages of butter and was back to my usual produce department duties. He had gone home to change into dry shoes and clean trousers, but his attitude was still one of embarrassment and anger directed at me. He said, "I can't afford you here anymore," and told me to, "Clock out and go home." The end of my first real job was a welcome relief. Even today, I would still laugh, knowing what was going to happen as a result of that laughter.

Dad's Chaw of Tobacco

I spent most of my working career in the hardware industry. One of my employers in that field was Belknap Hardware, the largest independent hardware wholesaler in the U.S. Once headquartered in downtown Louisville, Kentucky, it employed over 600 employees in an 11 story office/warehouse structure on property that went from Main Street, nearly down to the Ohio River. That building was blown up at the beginning of the movie, *Demolition Man,* starring Sylvester Stallone and Wesley Snipes.

It turns out, my dad also worked for Belknap when he was 17 years old, just prior to enlisting in the army for WWII. While working there, he always had a ready supply of chewing and smoking materials since my grandfather grew tobacco, as well as raised cattle, on his farm in Central Kentucky.

His immediate superior at Belknap, a foreman, discovered that my dad always had chewing tobacco on him and began regularly asking for a "chaw"—a small piece of tobacco big enough for chewing purposes. After awhile, my dad decided he was going to put an end to this guy's freeloading. He saved a "chaw" wrapped in cellophane paper in his pocket for just the right occasion.

When he saw his boss go into the restroom, he followed him in. Back then, the urinals were a big, long porcelain trough where he could stand right next to his boss. During the relieving process, my dad pulled out this "chaw" he had saved. He unwrapped it and put it where it could gather a bit of moisture. Then he wrapped it back in the cellophane and returned it to his pocket. His boss was shocked. He couldn't believe what he had just witnessed and asked my dad about what he had done.

My dad innocently responded with, "Didn't you know that's the best way to keep your tobacco moist?" That foreman never again asked for a chaw of tobacco.

Mealtime Grace

We lived near my aunt and uncle for most of my preteen years and celebrated all the holidays with them. My mother and father had divorced when I was two years old so we pretty much relied on my aunt's cooking during these occasions. In today's terms, we were a dysfunctional family. The adults were folks who smoked, drank, cussed, caroused and argued.

My aunt had fixed the food for our big Thanksgiving meal, but the drinking and arguing caused her to leave for a few hours. My uncle, who had drunk more than a few beers, decided we were going to have a proper holiday meal. So he sat all of us kids (seven with his five and my brother and me) down at the table and made sure we each had turkey and a selection of vegetables on our plates. Then he had second thoughts about eating and decided that a prayer of thanksgiving was needed.

He prayed. I don't remember what he said, but evidently he couldn't remember how to end the prayer. He paused to silently think about it and decided to say, "Ah-h-h, bye" a kind of amen/goodbye amalgamation. As soon as he said it, all we kids instantly burst into laughter at his hilarious boo-boo. One cousin within arm's reach felt my uncle's displeasure upside his head with a loud smack. He paid the price for all of us to have a never-to-be-forgotten holiday memory.

Honor Platoon

In May of 1969, I was drafted into the United States Armed Forces and was selected to serve in the Marine Corps. No one in my family had ever served as a marine, but I had read books about marines and heard stories so I knew this would be the experience of a lifetime. I wasn't scared but entered Marine Corps Recruit Depot, San Diego feeling apprehensive about what was going to happen.

I was 19 years old. I had grown up without a mom because of my parents' divorce when I was two. I was subjected to abusive cruelty by those who were paid to care for my brother and me while our dad worked. One lady broke a paddle ball paddle on my rear end in a zealous effort to make me become obedient. By the time I was in fifth grade, my stubbornness and rebellion caused the teachers in school to have me in a weekly rotation of spanking each day by a different teacher. By this time in life I had already built up a series of psychological walls to keep from getting hurt by others. Who knew that this would be excellent training for the physical and psychological techniques used by the Marine Corps drill instructors to transform normal human beings into outstanding marines?

The Marine Corps philosophy is to break down recruits mentally and physically, and then build them back up the Marine way. I already knew that physical pain was just a fleeting attempt at control and would quickly heal and be forgotten. I did learn that psychological punishment lasts much longer, sometimes even for a lifetime. I got my share of individual punishments and extra exercise, mostly for laughing at what the DI's were doing to some other poor soul who had messed up. There was also a whole lot of corporate punishment which obligated the whole platoon to engage in mental and physical activities designed to make us into a cohesive unit.

Training activities such as physical fitness tests, marching skills, rifle handling, qualifying at the range, hand-to-hand combat training and pugil stick training were graded on a point system within each company of four platoons. Platoon 2084, my platoon, placed second in every one of those events.

One day in our ninth week of training, our platoon commander and both DI's gathered our platoon into one Quonset hut, those corrugated metal buildings about 20 x 50 feet in diameter with a rounded shape. We were told to do push-ups, jumping jacks and squat thrusts in what soon became a sauna-like atmosphere—because early July in San Diego is hot! Nobody had a clue as to why we were being punished, but the platoon commander told us to ask the platoon guide what we had done. The platoon guide was the guy chosen by the platoon commander to carry the guidon, a pole with our platoon banner, in front of our platoon, every place we went.

He knew, but didn't know that he knew, because surely we weren't being punished for that! More exercises. This time we had to tuck our feet upon the top bunks and do push-ups on our knuckles. We were encouraged to ask the guide, "You dirty *****, what did we do?" We were to repeat this over and over while continuing to do push-ups on our knuckles. We had "fun" like this for about another hour. By then we were all soaked with sweat. Our field utility uniforms probably held five pounds of moisture. Finally, the platoon commander told us to tell the guide, "Thank you, you rotten bastard for not telling us we made honor platoon."

All of our second place position totals amounted to the best over-all score and so we would be flying the honor platoon banner on our guidon for the rest of our boot camp training. Immediately upon hearing this news, we stopped vilifying the guide. We all jumped to our feet, congratulating each other and hollering to the guide how sorry we were for treating him badly.

Staging Battalion

Just before going to Vietnam, marines go through Staging Battalion, the final training phase meant to acclimate you to where you are headed. At that point, the commanding officer (CO) for our company was a mustang officer; that means, he was an NCO (non-commissioned officer of corporal, E 4 or above rank) before going to Officers Candidate School (OCS). Mustangers came out of OCS with the rank of first lieutenant, instead of second lieutenant.

Our platoon commander, a staff sergeant whose most recent duty was training marines and sailors at "Seal" school, was on his way to Vietnam for his third tour of duty there. He carried a sawed off double barreled shotgun in a specially made holster on his right thigh and was one marine I did not hesitate to obey.

Our platoon sergeant was a really skinny guy with a huge Adam's apple and a little hitch in his walk like a small hesitation. When he walked, he reminded me of a chicken strutting its stuff. Coincidentally, at that time, the DJ, "Wolfman" Jack, was a hit on the local radio station and one of the characters on his show was called "Super Chicken." Whenever Wolfman Jack said, "Super Chicken," it was always followed by a high-pitched voice saying, "He's everywhere, he's everywhere!"

There were 80 or so guys in our platoon and, of course, my buddy Dallas and I were at the rear of first platoon. Naturally, we decided to have a little fun at the expense of our platoon sergeant. Whenever he gave a command to the platoon, Dallas would holler, "Super Chicken!" and I would follow with, "He's everywhere, he's everywhere," in a high pitched voice. We vehemently denied knowing what the sergeant was talking about when he accused us of this outrageous insult to him and his rank. After dealing with a few days of our rudeness, he complained to the platoon commander.

The platoon commander came to us and said he didn't care what we did at the back of the platoon; but he didn't want anyone to drop out of his platoon for any reason during our forced march training exercises. He placed the burden of this onto Dallas and me. He also said to have some fun but to ease up a bit on the platoon sergeant.

After that, if a guy got tired and slowed down during our forced marches, Dallas and I would carry his pack, M-60 machine gun, extra ammo belts or whatever, while pulling him along or pushing him up a hill. We'd also remind him of the platoon commander's admonition that he wanted no one to drop out of his platoon. At the same time, we implied that dire consequences from a guy who was a "Seal" instructor would befall any drop-out. Guys would soon catch their second wind, take back their gear and get back in their place, usually after we reached the top of the hill.

One Staging night was reserved for overnight bivouac, and, you might know, it rained that night. Murphy's Law! The temperature dropped rapidly from 85-90 down to 55-60 degrees Fahrenheit, and it felt freezing cold to us. (This was the only night it rained during the six months I spent in Southern California for training.)

Fortunately, Dallas and I had by this stage of our training abandoned water in our canteens in favor of Jack Daniels whiskey. We also loaded Twinkies, cheese crackers, Hostess Cupcakes and peanut butter sandwiches into our packs so we wouldn't have to eat C-rations, except for the canned fruit. We were trying to enjoy ourselves a bit during this time of sheer drudgery.

After a time of "fun and war games," during which some idiot in the armory mistakenly issued live ammo with tracers (every fifth round went off with a streak of red light when fired), the exercise was called off and we spent the rest of the night inside the grass roofed hooches of a simulated Vietnamese village. Thankfully, the CO and NCOs had pounded it into our heads to aim high, even when we thought we were using blank ammo. So nobody got hurt.

The platoon commander, with the CO in tow, found Dallas and me in one of the hooches about 3 a.m. and said he knew what we had in our canteens. My first thought was an expletive and that we were in deep doo-doo! I never did ask Dallas what he was thinking because the CO and the platoon commander both held out their canteen cups and said, "Pour." We spent the rest of the exercise sipping Jack Daniels and listening to stories from the two about Vietnam, the Marine Corps and life in general.

After that night, I had a new respect for superior officers and NCOs and for about what life in the Corps should be.

"Bad Moon Rising"

During the first six months of my tour of duty in Vietnam, the Commanding Officer of Lima Battery put me on Gun Number One as Assistant Crew Chief. This was a blatant attempt to allow Sgt. Cains (a by-the-book trained protégé of the gun platoon commander) to get me squared away as a marine. I was a Lance Corporal (E-3) at the time and reputed to have gone crazy in a non military-minded sort of way.

Gun One's hooch was right across the road from the officer's hooch and was supposed to help intimidate me into getting in line with Sergeant Cains' leadership. Sgt. Cains was a squared-away marine who regularly dressed in full olive drab utility uniform, polished his boots, and followed all the orders from his superiors. What his superiors didn't know was that underneath all that conformity was a real human being who needed to throw off that yoke of drabness and live a bit.

An ornery streak somewhere in the depths of my being intuitively knew what was wrong with Sgt. Cains and my new mission in life was born. I discovered Sgt. Cains' real first name was James, not Sgt., so I called him "Jimmy," with the rest of the Gun One crew following my lead. I convinced Jimmy that the crew needed to blow off steam every night to relieve the pressure of shooting the gun for hours at a time.

At 3 a.m. we'd compete in full contact football in our 16 x 32 foot plywood hooch built upon wooden 4 x 4's about 2 feet off the ground, while our stereo played at nearly full blast. One of our favorite songs was "We Gotta Get out of this Place" by Eric Burdon and the Animals. It was about a boy/girl relationship seeking the freedom of romance, but we liked that phrase about getting out "if it's the last thing we ever do," as it was repeated over and over in the refrain.

Another song we played over and over was "Bad Moon Rising," by Credence Clearwater Revival. Its words of warning pretty much captured our fear that we could die at any moment because death was as near as a sniper's bullet or a rocket lobbed in by the enemy. This song also had nothing to do with the Vietnam War, but it meshed with our mood and, more importantly, we knew it drove the "lifers" nuts!

Divine Intervention

About 18 months after my return from Vietnam, I was still angry at people, in general, for sending me off to war and then, upon my return, failing to recognize the sacrifices I had made. I was also angry at myself because I didn't like who I had become as a result of the war. I was even angry at God for letting yet another bad experience into my lonely life. Because I couldn't forget certain parts of the war, I ground my teeth at night and broke several in the process. This grinding continued for several more years until a peaceful life finally shut away those war experiences. In those early years, I also had a stomach ulcer; but drinking and partying were what my life had become. I dated many different young ladies and thought the one I was with would be the one I'd marry. But there was still something missing in my life. I had all this anger, even hatred, and no purpose to my life. I was ready to give up trying.

In an act of desperation, I went to a couple who had been in charge of the church youth group I was in before being drafted into the Marine Corps. Larry and Pat shared the story again about what Jesus had done for me at the cross. Later that night I knew it was either go with God or there was nothing for me; so I gave my life over to His service.

The next morning I told Larry and Pat what had happened. They wanted me to go to church regularly again, but I said I didn't fit in there anymore. They asked me to at least attend a Friday night Intervarsity Fellowship meeting during which college-age Christians gathered for volleyball, ping pong or other light sports and listened to a speaker on some religious topic; but I said I didn't really fit in there, either. Finally, just to please them, I agreed to go just once more on the next Friday evening.

I went alone to the Intervarsity meeting and only knew one guy from the few times I had attended in the years prior to being drafted. I told this young man at the end of the evening, "It was nice seeing you again, but I won't be back." What I didn't realize then was the effect of my meeting a young lady with light brown hair highlighted with a hint of blond from the summer sun.

We had sat beside each other on the grass, watching an old Laurel and Hardy movie, making small talk in-between the dialogue on screen. I managed to learn her name and that she was unattached; but it was her intelligence and beauty that kind of hit me between the eyes. In spite of what I told myself and my friend that first Friday evening, I felt compelled to be near and talk to that slim, lovely lady. We went for ice cream several weeks in a row with a group of others after the meeting. I finally worked up enough courage to ask her out on a real date. But when we went to see a movie of her choice, there was a line with more than a hundred people. Obviously we were not going to see the movie that night.

The next weekend our real first date was even worse. I thought we would go early to get the movie tickets, then eat and later see the movie. I drove a sharp looking pumpkin-colored Pontiac, less than a year old and since we were only buying the tickets, I pulled up right by the curb in front of the theater. After getting the tickets, I put my car in gear to drive away. Nothing happened. I shifted to park, back to drive and still no movement from my most prized possession. Upon opening my door and looking down, I saw a bright pink liquid running across the pavement from under my car. The seals on the transmission had chosen that very moment to quit doing their job, sabotaging my efforts to develop a relationship with this vision of loveliness.

We eventually saw the movie after one of her friends came and took us to get her red VW bug, allowing us to make it back to the theatre just before the movie started.

I still remember how small I felt sitting beside my date in the front seat of the tow truck—thinking I was dead in the water, sinking like a torpedoed ship, our relationship finished. I also remember how she took my breath away as she started down the aisle on our wedding day, escorted on her father's arm. And even now, after more than 38 years together, my heart still leaps when Claudia enters the room.

Christmas Stockings

No holiday was special or memorable for me during my growing-up years. I was ten years old before we got our own Christmas tree; prior to that we had all our holidays with my aunt and uncle's family. My uncle was Dad's brother. But their celebrations were not mine. It was *their*

Christmas tree, *their* Thanksgiving dinner, *their* Easter eggs to hunt. It felt like I was some useless appendage hanging off their family functions.

Holidays changed dramatically after I got married, especially after the children were born. Holidays were a lot of fun with all the preparations of food, decorations, costumes and presents. I would say this was all for the children, but I know inside that it was for me to experience all the holiday cheer and joy that I had desired as a child. I don't think we went crazy or extreme, but we did make sure our children got the latest trend in clothes, bedding (Spiderman sheets, for example) and toys like Big Wheel bikes, Sit-n-Spin and the Hungry, Hungry Hippo game.

Christmas stockings have been our big tradition. I never had one before my wife, Claudia, made one for each of us in the family. They were big with our names sewn in large white letters. They hung empty until early Christmas morning or after the children were asleep late on Christmas Eve. Each year there was a piece of fruit like an apple, orange or pear; nuts in the shell to be cracked; a new tooth brush; and chewing gum, candy treats and usually some variety of chocolate.

There was always another assortment of stuff that varied from year to year, depending on what little treats we stumbled upon during our shopping excursions. These were surprises for the children to discover deep in the toe of their stockings, items like match-box cars and action figures or, later, during their teen and adult years, video games, wallets and watches.

Even today with the children all in their thirties, we eagerly look forward to seeing what surprises have snuck into our Christmas stockings, hidden amongst the traditional menagerie of fruit, candy and gum.

Patricia Clark

Tricia is a Baby Boomer who began her journey in record-breaking heat in Brooklyn, New York. She grew up the middle of three sisters in a New York City suburb. Since then, she has lived in Maine, Puerto Rico, New York, France, South Carolina, Indiana, Ireland and Indiana again.

Her educational achievements include a diploma from the University of Clermont-Ferrand, France; a BA in Modern Languages from Clemson University; a BS in Computer Technology from Purdue University; and an M Ed in Instructional Design from Indiana University.

She has worked as a bilingual secretary, foreign language teacher, documentalist, computer programmer, technology training coordinator and technology recruiter.

Her peripatetic early adult life resulted in roots almost fifteen years deep in Indiana. She enjoys cooking, reading, travel, movies and theatre. She treasures the experiences of the places she has been and fervently hopes her journey leads to many more places in the future.

Confessions of a Good Girl, or Vote, Vote for Miss Rheingold!

My mother's hair was thick and dark auburn, and for a while she wore it in a style that I think of as "I want a more glamorous life"—shoulder-length waves, parted on the side, with a lock not quite covering one eye. The young Lauren Bacall copied her style almost exactly, as far as I could tell from the rare issue of *Photoplay* magazine that crossed my six-year-old path.

I didn't have any hair at all until well into my third year. This chagrined my mother deeply, especially since the firstborn (my older sister) came into the world with a full head of black hair. So much hair that it had to be pinned back out of her eyes when she was only months old. My mother got tired and frustrated of accepting the praise of strangers cooing over "your precious boy" and would have been ecstatic, I'm sure, to have lived in a later time when bald baby girls can wear little elastic bands around their heads with a bow or flower attached and spare their mothers this heartache.

My complexion favors the Scots Irish of my mother's side and not the Dutch/German/Cuban of my father's, and when my hair finally showed up, it was a slightly lighter auburn. By that time, my little sister had been born and my mother would proudly report to anyone who would listen that she had "a blonde, a brunette and a redhead."

I was born way too soon for doll diversity, so with the exception of Raggedy Ann, dolls had blonde hair. Blonde curls were the sine qua non of feminine kid beauty in my day, a standard that extended from the beloved Toni Home Perm doll Santa brought me one year to the Shirley Temple reruns that I watched on "Million Dollar Movie." Lacking the requisite color, I got the ringlets by way of the bobby pin-held pin curls my mother would create on Saturday nights after washing my hair in preparation for Sunday church.

Sunday was a big day at our house. Lunch was our main meal and dinner was always more or less the same: Campbell's soup and sandwiches made with cold meats and salads from the deli served on Kaiser rolls, with a cake or pastries from the bakery. The businesses in our town were closed, so after church my father would drive two towns over to go to the deli and bakery for our treats. Sometimes I'd go along for the ride and the chance to have input into the week's choices. If we were going visiting that afternoon, we'd get an extra cheesecake as a hostess gift and we'd get something wonderful for ourselves—maybe a cheesecake, or éclairs thick with pastry cream filling, or napoleons so high they wouldn't fit in your mouth or Italian butter cookies in the colors of the rainbow.

Our first stop was the deli. The phrase "New York deli" is like a code for anyone who has experienced one. It is a singular place, selling not only the quotidian things we knew, but foods from all over the world with their strange sounding names and smells of ethnicity. One product sold was Rheingold Beer. According to Wikipedia:

Rheingold is a New York beer that held 35 percent of the state's beer market from 1950 to 1960. At the center of its media campaign was the "Miss Rheingold" pageant. Beer drinkers voted each year on the young lady who would be featured as Miss Rheingold in advertisements. In the 1940s and 1950s in New York, the selection of Miss Rheingold was as highly anticipated as the race for the White House. The company's headquarters was in the Bushwick section of Brooklyn.

My father's allegiance to Rheingold may have been that of a homesick Canarsie boy relocated to the suburbs, or maybe he was simply one of "a loyal cadre of workingmen who would just as soon have eaten nails as drink another beer maker's suds," as described by the *New York Times*. Although I've seen advertisements that contradict memory, *I* remember the Miss Rheingold yearly candidate lineup as a brunette, two blondes and a redhead. And, conforming to life as I knew it, the winner was *always* one of the blondes.

On one of those Sunday trips, I realized you didn't actually have to be a beer *drinker* to vote for Miss Rheingold. Ballots and voting boxes were in every deli in the area as well as in bars. The counter help was too busy to monitor who voted and how often. So, nonchalantly taking about ten ballots from the tear-off display, I voted over and over for the redhead. For weeks afterward, I was a regular on those Sunday trips: a woman (in training) with a mission and the sure knowledge that if I voted enough times, the course of advertising beauty pageant history would be irrevocably changed.

I was raised to be a good girl and did really well at it. As a child I rarely got in trouble, and I don't remember ever getting spanked. Maybe the true rebellion was being stored up for manifestations that would come later in my life. That said, the frisson of disobedience I felt on Sundays during the years I stuffed the Rheingold ballot boxes in the certain knowledge that *this* would at last be The Year of The Redhead showed me that I didn't always have to walk a straight, prescribed line, that I could bend some rules and the sky would not fall in, that repeated disappointment doesn't have to result in disillusionment and defeat—it can be a paving stone on the road to strength and independence.

In Tribute: Miss Rheingold Girls 1940-1965, Hair Color Unknown to Me (I'm betting blonde)

1940 Jinx Falkenburg; 1941 Ruth Ownbey; 1942 Nancy Drake; 1943 Sonia Gover; 1944 Jane House; 1945 Pat Boyd; 1946 Rita Daigle; 1947 Michaele Fallon; 1948 Pat Quinlan; 1949 Pat McElroy; 1950 Pat Burrage; 1951 Elise Gammon; 1952 Anne Hogan; 1953 Mary Austin; 1954 Adrienne Garrett; 1955 Nancy Woodruff; 1956 Hillie Merritt; 1957 Margie McNally; 1958 Madelyn Darrow; 1959 Robbin Bain; 1960 Emily Banks; 1961 Janet Mick; 1962 Kathy Kersh; 1963 Loretta Rissell; 1964 Celeste Yarnall; 1965 Sharon Vaughn

The House on Washington Street

You crossed a railroad viaduct on the walk from downtown Winchester, Kentucky to my grandparents' house. Passenger trains as well as freights were still running into the early 60s—the last time I spent summers in Winchester with my mother and sisters. As a grade-schooler in the mid-1950s, I remember how if we timed our return correctly, the trains' vibrations would upset the delicate balance of the five-scoop ice cream cones we bought at Duff's Drug Store and ate on the way home.

Duff's was on the side of Main Street where the shops were at sidewalk level, and not three steps up from the street. My mother had worked there as a teenager and again as a young widow. Our East Coast sophisticated selves were pleasantly surprised to learn that you could get scrumptious fountain treats at a *drug store,* since there were no candy stores in town. Even more delightful was the discovery that ice cream was five cents a scoop. My weekly allowance covered that five scoop cone, whereas at home in New York, it only bought a one-scooper. The fact that I often came back wearing most of the ice cream on my seersucker blouse or shorts, or that I may have sacrificed a scoop or two to the train did not diminish my pleasure one bit.

The wraparound porch at my grandparents' contained entire worlds for us. On rainy days, we went "fishing" off the railing. As far as I knew, fish came from: the A&P (sticks, cans of tuna and salmon); the butcher (cakes on Friday); or as shrimp brought home on the Long Island Railroad, wrapped in brown paper tied with a string and carried by my father from the Fulton Market by its wooden handle. Did I really believe I might catch something off the porch? I think I did.

My cousin Fara was the creative organizer of the shows we presented on the porch. As tiny and pixyish as I was tall and awkward, she could always talk us into some elaborate sing along or show of dancing and cheering prowess, complete with home-made costumes. Her size made her the expert hider when we played hide and seek in the snowball bushes in the front yard after dinner. We trapped generations of fireflies in our mayonnaise jars, humanely trying to keep them alive by including some grass in their prisons and poking air holes in the jar lids.

The house was two stories—a parlor, dining room, kitchen and back porch downstairs; bedrooms that smelled of un-air-conditioned southern summers up. The wringer washing machine, an instrument of the devil that endlessly fascinated me and painfully nipped my fingertips more than once, was on the closed-in back porch. On washdays, the humid smells of detergent and bluing and the *chug chug* of modern life in action spread throughout the house.

The white gingerbread porch gave a touch of beauty and elegance to the house on Washington Street. It was a place of freedom for all of us. The daily rules—bed times, what we could eat and do, where we could go by ourselves—were relaxed. My mother relaxed as well. It seems to me now as though she held her breath in New York and finally exhaled and became her real self again when she was with her family and old friends in July and August. She, and by extension, *we* were always welcomed as though we had just left the day before. We were not guests but cherished family. Her southern accent, long since lost, *always* came back within the first week of our visits. Or so my sisters and I teased.

"Hello Darkness, My Old Friend"—December 1966, Orono, Maine

My son was born at the end of the first semester of my sophomore year in college. I was 19 and his father (a senior) was 21. We lived in an area of summer cottages that were rented as student housing during the school year. "Cottage" was a term that covered a lot of ground in this enclave—one of our friends lived in what amounted to a studio house with no shower or tub. Not long before Chris arrived, we moved to a house on the top of the hill and into the relative lap of luxury—a flush toilet (not chemical like at our old place) a gas (not wood-burning) stove for cooking, a large living room with a picture window that looked out over the Bangor River and a bedroom big enough for a bassinette. We struggled with finances and classes and responsibilities, but I was certain once David finished his degree and got a job, everything would be fine. We might be young, and I might be lost in a kind of poetic internal life many days, scored by Joni Mitchell and Judy Collins and Simon and Garfunkel, but our love and marriage were forever. Somehow we'd get the hang of being grown up.

Was anyone ever less ready to be a mother than I? Or more frightened? "Young and dumb" is how I describe that "me." I was fully aware of the biology, yet still asked, "Are you sure?" when I was told it was a boy. Somehow, since I'm the middle of three girls, the idea that I would bear a son never crossed my mind. Chris was a healthy, full-term newborn whom I was certain would either starve to death or die of SIDS. Not only were we not snowed in (as I feared) it was sunny and in the high 50s the December Friday he was born. As he slept, I'd pray for him to wake up and even put my finger under his nose to make sure he was still breathing, and when he was crying for some unfathomable (to me) reason, I'd pray for him to go to sleep. I could see bears in the woods from miles and miles away, and if they weren't there, I'd see them anyway.

"How do you do this? I can't!" I panicked over and over. Even with my own mother and grandmother as excellent role models, and with helpful friends and neighbors, I felt inept—isolated, lonely, unsure, apart. No one I knew had a baby so young. No one knew my struggles, the weight of responsibility. I had no words to describe my feelings, as verbal as I am.

Someone, maybe in a prenatal class or well-baby clinic, told me that keeping your baby in the center of your life and not catering to it too much in terms of quiet and routine would be a good thing. The baby would be more adaptable and less fussy. Maybe I simply wanted to believe this since the crib wouldn't fit in the bedroom and *had* to go in the living room. So we had parties and played music and people came and went. I carried on many conversations with Chris as he sat in his baby swing and I did my homework at the kitchen table. Our single friends were amazed at how "modern" David and I were to manage all this. My silent response was "You make your decisions and then you live with them. You do what you have to do."

Simon and Garfunkel's album, *Parsley, Sage, Rosemary and Thyme*, particularly its song, "Sounds of Silence," became my anthem of anxiety, loneliness and hope. I thought the downbeat story reflected my own reality: serious and introspective, a little oblique. An unlikely lullaby from an accidental mother. In truth, I don't really know why it has always affected me so deeply. But when I hear it, I am that young woman with all her dreams and insecurities. My future was in the living room and out there someplace. If I worked hard and got lucky, my deep love for my son would give me the maternal instincts I seemed bereft of, and my devotion to him and honoring of my life responsibilities would see us through.

David got a job and I became a faculty wife, in Puerto Rico no less, at the age of 20. We were divorced before Chris turned three. Although I thought the world had ended, it only tilted for a bit, and then I slowly picked myself up and built another life for Chris and myself. It was the beginning of my education as to who I am and what I'm capable of doing.

The baby in the crib in the living room will be 45 this December. He has been married for 20 years and is the father of two sons, 12 and 8. He works as a school district administrator in California. I say he turned out well despite my best efforts. To this day, he can sleep anywhere at any time.

Groupe Scolaire Jean Butez

From late December 1972 through late November 1974, I lived with my husband and son in Clermont-Ferrand, an industrial city in Central France. Martin's job with Michelin Tire brought us to a place the French referred to as *triste* (sad) due to its many factories and dearth of green space. I was thrilled to be there. Something about French life, even in a provincial city—the formality, the food, the differences obvious and subtle in language, lifestyle, shopping, seemingly *everything* suited me very well. Walking upstairs from the ground floor to the first, second and finally to our large third floor apartment, I felt as though I was truly in my place and hoped I could stay forever.

My son, Chris, had his sixth birthday a few weeks before our relocation. In New York, he had been in kindergarten, and we were able, with the help of the Michelin Personnel Service, and over the objections of the school staff, to enroll him in a local *maternelle* for his first six months of school. *Maternelle* is an advanced form of American pre-school, and the idea that a six year old would attend *maternelle* was unheard of. Thankfully, he got those months to learn some French and his way around a foreign schoolyard. With time, his American winter jacket became less and less strange and so less of a source of teasing, and I learned where to buy the "right" kind of *tablier* (smock) so he wouldn't stick out from the rest of class.

By the time Chris started first grade in September 1973, Michelin had opened a school for the children of its expat community with an American curriculum and teachers from the States. The grade school hours were 8:30 – 11:30 a.m. Some families kept their children at home the other part of the day, but by then I was enrolled as a foreign student at the university and so from 1:30-4:30 p.m. on Monday, Tuesday, Thursday and Friday, and on Saturday morning, Chris attended Groupe Scolaire Jean Butez, the public school across two streets and around two corners from our apartment.

To my amazement and delight, Chris loved this arrangement and thrived through hard work and a little help from me. To this day, I can recall bits of some of the French poems he had to memorize and recite. I see him walking down the stairs, backpack filled with notebooks and a slate and chalk, on his way to learn to read and do math in a second language at the same time he was learning these same things in his first. Once a week, he was allowed to stop at the *patisserie* that he passed on the way home from school and buy a pastry for his afternoon snack. As an incentive, I always made sure he had enough money to buy anything in the shop. "If you can ask for it in French, you can have it" was our agreement. He fairly quickly settled on *pain au chocolat* (chocolate croissant) and *chausson aux pommes* (apple turnover) as his regular choices.

This was our school routine for all of Chris' first grade, and his second grade from September to late November 1974. Although he lost most of his language fluency over time, we tease that he always managed to raise his G.P.A. in high school and college by taking yet another French class.

Before Martin died, he and I returned to Clermont-Ferrand on a vacation with Chris when he was 15. He was 44 this past June when my husband Jesse and I went there on another vacation, this time with Chris and his family (his wife and two sons, 12 and 8.) We had a lot to celebrate in 2011: their 20th anniversary, our 15th anniversary and my continuing recovery from breast cancer.

Clermont-Ferrand has sprawled outward over the years. The close in suburbs and farther out towns where some of our American compatriots chose to live and needed two cars to cope with that decision, are now connected to the city center by a tram system and a light rail. During the day, it's pay parking on the square across from our old apartment building. The *pétanque* (bocce, boules) field at one end of the square is still in use, although the old men in their *bleus de travail* work overalls who we often watched in the 70s are probably gone. The sporting association built a clubhouse for the "boulers" sometime in our absence that looks very spacious and permanent. The factories are still there making tires of many types and sizes and spewing carbon black into the air. I wonder if whoever lives in our old apartment still has to contend with dark streaks on the windows.

Our grandsons have seen their father's first grade class picture many times. It's easy to pick him out—obeying the command to sit up straight, blond hair a contrast to the dark locks of the children of our neighbors, the guest workers from Portugal and Turkey as well as the French. When we all walked from outside our building to the school one early evening in late June, some of our memories reflected the present, some didn't. The *patisserie* is still where it was, although it has been remodeled. Many of the other stores are different from what I remember. The school looks the same and in memory I could see the students lined up in pairs to go back inside to their lessons after a time in the play-yard, quieting at the teacher's orders and preparing to return to class. The boy who so bravely adapted to and then thrived in a life far from what he had known is who he is now in part because of his long ago experiences.

I am happy to have been able to take another walk to school—this time with my true love, son, daughter-in-law and grandsons. I am grateful for the changes in me that came from my time in France and thankful I was able to share my memories at their source with all the people who mean the most to me.

On the Train

For his entire career, my father worked as the bookkeeper for an electrical supply company in lower Manhattan. Beginning in the 1930s, when he lived in Brooklyn, he commuted by subway. When he used the G.I. Bill to move my mother, my sisters and me to the suburbs in the early 1950s, he got to work on the Long Island Railroad, changing at Jamaica Station and continuing from there to his office by a different subway line. Although he looked nothing like "Dashing Dan," the personification of LIRR's dashing commuter, he was a loyal monthly ticketholder until the day he retired in the late 1970s.

I took "The Route of the Dashing Commuter" to work when I returned to New York at 22 with a not-quite-three year old in tow. Thanks to having spent the previous two years as a faculty wife in Puerto Rico, I was able to get a real job in the international division of Helena Rubinstein Cosmetics.

This was the 1960s, and there was a certain elegance to commuting in those days. For an additional charge, you could sit in the club car, where uniformed waiters served cocktails as wealthy businessmen sat in club chairs and smoked. For everyone else, there was a bar car where you could stand at small tables and enjoy a drink on your way home.

My workweek was split between the "lipstick factory," where I told my son I went each day, a 20 minute drive from the town I lived in, and the corporate offices in the General Motors building on 5th Avenue at 59th Street. The commute was LIRR to Jamaica, change trains for Penn Station, and get a 7th Avenue uptown subway to the 50's and walk from there. I went to the city two days a week so that my boss, Jorge, would not have to come to the factory. I dashed so he could keep his rent controlled apartment and his after work gig playing at a piano bar on the Upper West Side.

Jorge was so thankful that I agreed to this arrangement that most days I was on my way home well before the crush of other commuters. One day, however, my father and I agreed to meet at Jamaica on the 5:28 and ride the rest of the way to Syosset together. We planned to meet in the bar car, since it was the most easily located at that rush hour.

When I arrived, my father was already there. He greeted me, and as the train left the station, asked me if I would like a drink.

I said, "Yes, I would. The Rubinstein Crazies were in rare form today, going on and on about various styles of false eyelashes and I'm tired."

"What would you like?" he asked. My father was not a big drinker—he took a drink at Christmas, Easter and

Thanksgiving and had a beer or three the rest of the year and I can't imagine that a stop in the bar car was part of his regular trip home. When my life exploded and I had to live with my parents for most of the year after I got divorced, he helped clean out the bedrooms and move me and my son in. He also had the absolute ability to turn me into a nine year old until he died when I was 51.

So, I made the only possible response for a nine year old: "What can I have?"

"You can have what you want," he replied.

That night in 1970, in the bar car of the Long Island Railroad, I ordered and drank a Bloody Mary in front of God and the rest of the dashing commuters. I don't remember what my father had, although I do remember toasting the end of the workday. What I remember most was my feeling of hard won victory: without saying a word, my father told me that he knew I was an adult who was handling my situation as well as I could and that he believed I could do it.

Bill Culley

Bill first saw the light of day in Peoria, Illinois and attended grade schools there until the sixth grade at which time he was transformed from an urban dweller into a novice farm boy.

After graduating from high school, he was eager to pursue a life in the field of chemistry and followed his grandmother's sage advice of joining the army to get the GI Bill. He was stationed near Baltimore, and frequently had the chance to travel to New York City to see Broadway plays. He still maintains an interest in the theatre.

After the army, he obtained his B.S. degree at Bradley University in chemistry and then completed his Ph.D. in biochemistry at Purdue followed by an enjoyable career in the study of genetic diseases. After retirement in 1991, he taught chemistry at IUPUI on a part-time basis for ten years.

He is blessed with two wonderful children, Bonnie and Connie, several very nice stepchildren and a flock of grandchildren. He spends many joyful nights skipping around the ballroom dance floor, and during the day he is entertained by his work on the computer. He is pleased to be able to hone his writing skills in the current class.

The Pony

Ever since the first grade when a gentleman stopped by our house offering brief pony rides for 25 cents, which included the wearing of a cowboy hat, I yearned for a pony of my own. The chances of my being able to ride off into that wonderful fantasy land of roaming the Wild West on my pony seemed pretty remote, but my grandmother had a way of making even the remote come to life. I was in the third grade and it was my birthday. I was suddenly pulled into another world when a truck slowly came to a stop carrying the most gorgeous pony I had ever seen. This majestic, brown and white pony pranced around on the truck and whinnied loud and clear that she was eager for me to climb aboard and ride off into the sunset. Could it be that this pony was really for me? Had the fantasy that was my last thought each night really come true? My grandmother lived a pretty simple and modest life, but she worked miracles to make my life exciting.

Grandma looked like a picture you would expect to find in any album of early twentieth century photos. Her neatly curled hair was pinned tightly against her head. She wore a modest amount of makeup, a little rouge and lipstick, but wouldn't dream of wearing anything like eye shadow or other adornments. Her dress with a modest design was a couple of inches below her knees. I never saw her in anything but a dress—no slacks or, heaven forbid, shorts of any kind. I can't imagine my grandmother even wearing a bathing suit. I never heard her raise her voice, although my mother and she on several occasions had strong disagreements about which was worse: losing your husband by death or divorce? My grandmother was divorced and my mother lost my father by death. Each thought theirs was by far the greater burden to bear.

My grandmother had little confidence in herself. Even though everyone who knew her said she was the finest seamstress they had ever seen, she always expressed doubt that she could do a very good job whenever anybody asked her to sew something. Her fine dresses of all sorts, even wedding dresses, were always perfect. My mother tells the story of Grandma successfully applying for a job as a seamstress in the most elite fur store in Peoria and expressing amazement that they hired her, commenting, "I guess they just hire anyone."

Although she lived a simple, conservative sort of life, my grandma had a keen sense of humor and enjoyed playful activities. I don't think I ever went to my grandmother's house in my early years without her bouncing me on her knees. I would sit facing her on her lap, fall backward and she would catch me. We would do this over and over again. This was more fun than any video game ever invented. She also enjoyed telling me stories about how the horses ran amuck when the first cars came chugging down the streets in Argos, Indiana and about her grandparents discussing the hardships of the Civil War days. She was a wizard at finding practical gifts for me that I didn't even know I needed until she gave them to me. One was a fur display from 20 different animals that I took to school on several occasions for show and tell. And I am sure I was the only kid in town who had an outfit of real leopard fur just like Tarzan wore. My goal of going to college to study chemistry seemed pretty farfetched, but it was my grandmother who brought me the ad in the paper about serving in the army to get something called the GI Bill.

As if a pony wasn't enough, my grandmother made some chaps as good as any in the Wild West and a cowboy hat that transformed me into the Gene Autry of Thrush Street, the fastest draw in the West. I named my pony Ginger because she was full of it. I must have inherited some sort of gene from my father that carried us off into the fantasy land of the great Wild West. He often told stories of his father being a sheriff somewhere in Oklahoma and the heroics that were a part of his life. In my younger years, I thought my grandfather had single handedly tamed the West. I'm sure my dad's stories were embellished a bit, maybe a lot, but they were interesting and he loved to tell them. Time and time again. I knew them by heart. The fantasy gene was a bit diluted in my case and disappeared as I reached adulthood although, I must admit, as a teenager I sometimes visualized myself as the unheralded player in some heroic role like winning the game by catching a touchdown pass in the closing seconds of the game.

Ginger provided me with many years of fun as I rode her bareback to far and distant places. She was always eager to go and was off to the races whenever we turned for home. I went on many a ride down dusty roads seeking out the villains that were terrorizing the town folks. On days when I was more in touch with reality, there were the more mundane things to do like feeding my steed and cleaning up the horse manure or, more correctly, the pony manure. After a good and faithful life, Ginger bit the dust like many other gallant rides before her, but my memories of her live on as do the memories of my grandma who gave me many wonderful gifts, the greatest of which was her presence in my life.

Cousin Bob's Visit

It had been a quiet day, and we were just sitting down to dinner when Mom glanced out the window and anxiously exclaimed, "Oh Lord, it's Bob and his family."

Dad dejectedly responded, "Oh God."

By this time Bob and his wife, Mary, and the baby had gotten out of the front of the truck and the rest of the thirteen children had jumped out of the back of the truck, and they were all parading up to the house. Bob never called ahead to see if it was a convenient time for him to visit. He just showed up with his wife and 13 children, and you never knew when he was going to leave. That meant he might be staying overnight. He did not need an invitation, and he did not take hints about it being an inconvenient time. He was a pleasant enough fellow and his children were well behaved, but that is a lot of people and a lot of disruption in a small home consisting of a kitchen, a living room and two bedrooms.

Dad had one sibling, a sister named Nancy. His dad had died when he was 16 and he quit high school to support his mother and sister. Even though Dad was bringing in the money for the family, he angrily related to me on several occasions that Nancy frequently complained that she wasn't getting her share of his income. I never heard him get into an argument with Nancy, but he did his best to avoid her. Mom says she didn't think Nancy ever dated until she met John. After a short period of dating, they decided to get married. Mom tells about Nancy receiving a diaphanous nightie at her wedding shower and exclaiming, "Oh no, John will be able to see right through it." Well, apparently he did. Exactly nine months after they were married, they had their first child. That was Bob.

Bob and his family had arrived in a big farm truck with the kids riding in the back. The truck served as the family vehicle and also as the vehicle for farm duties like taking livestock to market. They led a pretty primitive lifestyle, purchasing only a few staples like flour and sugar at the store. His wife, Mary, made all of the clothes for the family, mostly work clothes but also one outfit for going to church for each member of the family. They had a large garden and raised livestock for meat. In addition, they liked wild game and frequently hunted for deer, squirrel, rabbit, turkey and one of their favorites, possum. Bob sometimes brought a dish of possum to the annual family reunion. It might have been delicious, but not many chose to try it. Bob ended up taking most of his possum home with him.

Mary and the kids hung around the house that day, while Bob spent part of the day at a local garage because of some problem he was having with his truck. As the sun began to go down, they were making no effort to leave and were hinting about staying all night. Mom explained that we just didn't have accommodations for them, and Bob replied that they could all just sleep on the floor in the living room wherever they fell asleep. The next morning the living room was a disaster. Mary had left wet diapers on the hardwood floor and Mom nearly had a stroke. There were kids and clothes everywhere, but all of Bob's family were just lounging around, calm, cool and collected. Mom fixed everyone a hearty breakfast, and they were on their way by noon that day.

Mom visited their home sometime after that and found they indeed lived a very primitive life in an environment of controlled turmoil, even though everyone worked hard and got along pretty well. The most shocking experience that Mom had was when she asked about the toilet facilities and Bob pointed out toward the back. She looked around outside, and when she did not see an outhouse, she went back inside to tell Bob. Bob replied, "Just go anywhere." Mom wasn't accustomed to just going anywhere and found the instructions very troublesome. Mom never explained to me why they had no outhouse at that time, if indeed she knew. That was the last time that she visited Bob's home.

Bob and Mary have both passed on now and their thirteen children have all grown to become solid citizens and more refined than their dad. As I reflected on this, I thought, "Bob, you did a good job."

The Untold Story

Dad loved to get together with almost any group to tell stories, and he told many of them time and time again. As he told them, he was reliving the incident, telling it with great fervor. He would laugh out loud at some of the humorous parts, as if he had never heard them before. Acquaintances of his who had heard the stories many times were tolerant because he seemed to be having such a good time telling them. His enthusiasm was contagious. I soon learned to be very careful about information I shared with him that he might think everybody in town should know, with some colorful embellishments, of course. This was particularly true of any dates that I had. For example, once I could drive a car and could date, Dad was telling virtually anyone who would listen, "Bill is spending too much time with that Natzky girl and not getting all of his farm work done." She confronted me in due time and asked where she stood on my priority list. With some stumbling around, I was finally able to convince her that there was time for her and my farm work.

Dad was pretty demanding and expected work to get done right the first time when he assigned me tasks. He was not tolerant of errors in my farm work or when I didn't get assigned tasks completed. He could be loud and clear when he was unhappy with me, but he never disciplined me in a physical manner. Whenever I didn't get the amount of assigned field work done, he would remind me of the importance of finishing it in a timely manner so the crops would be ready when it was time to harvest. Dad was working at Caterpillar Tractor Company so most of the field work was my responsibility.

In my junior year, some of the other basketball players and I decided it would be fun to drive over to Elmwood, a nearby town, to see the basketball game since the two teams playing would be opponents of ours later in the season. Though I knew that I was not supposed to drive out of town, I volunteered to do so, thinking this would raise my stature with the gang. Surprisingly, I was not very nervous about taking the car out of town even though I knew that there would be a price to pay if I was caught. Driving fast for no good reason seemed to be the rule of the day. It was more daring and exciting. We took off for Elmwood down a gravel road that I was not familiar with at a speed that was way faster than necessary, and it was very dark outside. Suddenly, one of the guys yelled, "There's a crook in the road. We're not going to make it!" As I tried to make the turn, the car began to roll over and over.

Once it stopped, we were upside down and at a strange angle. It was pitch black. I was anxious, but not visibly upset at that moment. I yelled, "Is everyone all right?" One of the guys said, "Dave is bleeding like a stuck pig." Everyone was able to climb out of the car, but we were a little disoriented because we were in unfamiliar territory and couldn't even see our hand in front of our face. We saw lights in a farmhouse and were able to walk there, although Dave had trouble from a badly cut knee. We called the police, and they were there shortly and took Dave to the hospital and the rest of us home. I felt guilty about the injury to Dave because of my recklessness. I was feeling more anxious at this point as I contemplated what the consequences would be for this escapade which topped the list when it came to defying authority and the consequences that were sure to follow.

When I returned home, I woke up Mom and timidly and remorsefully told her what had happened. Her first concern was to make sure I was all right. She looked me in the eye and said, "You know your dad is going to be home in about an hour and you're going to have to explain this whole thing to him." At this point I was visibly upset, very anxious and contemplating how pitiful I could make myself look with the few scratches and bruises I had.

Dad was riding home from work with a friend, and I heard them pulling into the driveway. The car door slammed shut. Soon Dad stepped in and said, "How are you doing, Bill? Did you have a good evening? I didn't see the car out there when I came in."

I sheepishly and nervously told him what had happened. To my amazement, he rather calmly asked, "Are you all right?" Feigning injuries just did not seem like the right thing to do at this point. I deserved whatever punishment that I received. After a moment, my Dad said calmly and directly, "You know this is going to be a hardship on the family. We cannot afford another car like that. It was nice to have a car here at the house for running errands for your mother, but she'll have to get by without that for awhile. I'm grateful that you were not injured."

At this point, I was feeling like the most undeserving and irresponsible person on earth. Where were all of the yelling and harsh words I had expected? That would have made it so much easier. As much as Dad loved to tell stories, I never heard him tell any about this incident.

"When It's Springtime in the Rockies"

Mom and Dad lived in Denver for some time in the 1920s so I guess it should be no surprise that one of my Dad's two favorite songs was "When It's Springtime in the Rockies." The other song he loved was "Let Me Call You Sweetheart." That was pretty much the extent of his repertoire, but he sang them often and with gusto. Even though Mom was a cheerful soul, she never sang around the house. That was Dad's domain and he cherished it. The melody was not always recognizable, but he made up for it by singing loudly and with intensity. I can remember those two songs from my earliest preschool years.

Recordings of "When it's Springtime in the Rockies" were typically made by western personae like Gene Autry, Slim Whitman and Tex Ritter, which I am sure added to the mystique of the song since Dad loved the lore of the Wild West. He was always immersed in a western novel, Zane Grey being one of his favorite authors. When he was working the evening shift at Caterpillar Tractor Company, he would get home from work about midnight and often read until two or three in the morning or until Mom would come out and say, "Tom, it's time to go to bed." Those novels simply transported him into another world. Mom could stand right in front of his chair and say, "Tom, dinner is ready," and he would remain fixed in his western world, truly not hearing a word that she had said.

"When It's Springtime in the Rockies" was copyrighted in 1923, and since Mom and Dad moved to Denver in the mid-1920s, it was no doubt a pretty popular song in that era. In 1937, the song was featured in a Gene Autry movie titled, *When It's Springtime in the Rockies*, that pitted the sheepherders against cattlemen in the American West. Betty Grable starred in a romantic caper in 1942 that featured the song and also was the title of the movie. The romantic lyrics by Mary Hale Woolsey and Milt Taggert and the musical score by Robert Sauer have remained appealing though the years.

Whenever I hear this song, which is not often, I think of Dad and the joy he had singing it. I picture him hanging out in heaven with Gene Autry and the rest of the gang, singing away on the trail and telling stories of the Wild West. When someone would tell a story, Dad would frequently say, "I can tell you one better than that." He wasn't intending to be rude and the thought never occurred to him that he might be offending anyone. He simply thought his story was better. I'm sure he is up there telling Gene and the gang, "I can tell you one better than that."

My New Life as a Dancer

I was more than a little anxious as I made the hour's drive that September Sunday from the small town where I lived to the big city of Indianapolis. I had made the drive many times, but this evening was a new undertaking, one that I had prepared for, but now I had my doubts about. Surely, the three months of preparation in learning the foxtrot, the swing and other dances would at least be adequate, so I would blend into the crowd. I would soon know.

As I approached the YWCA where the Continental Dance Club held their dance each Sunday, I noticed a large number of cars already parked. This was no small affair. The building was shabby from the outside and clearly had seen better days. As I entered, I noticed that it was not air-conditioned. Already, the evening was off to a bad start. I've always perspired freely and being nervous in a building that was not air-conditioned was not going to be good. The interior was in need of painting; the restrooms were not well maintained; the blinds were askew with beams of light peaking through at a variety of points; and the dance floor was well worn. The tables had folding legs, and there were folding chairs around them. In spite of the shortcomings of the facility, it was clear from the crowd of people joyfully chatting with each other that they liked dancing there.

This was different from the sheltered environment of a dance studio. I had no reason to believe that I would know anyone here, and that, indeed, turned out to be the case. During the lesson that preceded the dance, it was evident to me, and, I'm sure to everyone else, that I wasn't a seasoned dancer. By now, I was very anxious and perspiring. Everyone was catching on to the dance steps more quickly than me. I was glad when the lesson was over.

There was a 30-minute break between the lesson and the dance. I chose an empty table at which to sit, and soon three lovely ladies who had not been at the lesson walked toward my table. They were pleasantly chatting and had nice smiles. I thought, "Wow, maybe I'll get a chance to dance with them. I'll keep it simple and only do the steps that I can do fairly well." As luck would have it, they sat right down at my table. I was saying to myself, "Thank you, God." Even at 61 years of age, I was a bit anxious about meeting them and, in particular, dancing with them. Were they going to be super-duper dancers that would cause me to look glaringly incompetent? I was eager to make a good impression. They seemed eager to talk, and we were soon carrying on a comfortable conversation. At least the talking was going okay.

It was great to see that a live band would be playing. I much preferred that to CDs. I love the big band music of Glen Miller, Tommy Dorsey and others that is frequently played at dances. As old standards from the '40s and '50s are performed, I frequently find myself warmly reminiscing about what was going on in my life when the song being played became popular. "Sentimental Journey" and "Dream" are two of my favorites from my senior prom.

The music started. It was time to dance. During the first few songs, I asked each of the three ladies to dance. They were all better dancers than me, but they were very tolerant of my limited abilities. I became more at ease as the evening wore on, and they at least appeared to be enjoying dancing with me. What a surprise!

I was particularly attracted to the tallest of the three ladies. Mary made comfortable conversation, had a trim figure, a stately bearing, dark brown eyes, shoulder length wavy blonde hair, and an ever-present smile. She was gorgeous. I loved dancing with her. She seemed to float across the floor, seemingly unaware that I wasn't dancing equally well. In addition to our love for dancing, we had other common interests. She enjoyed going to plays and was an avid bridge player.

What a wonderful evening. Time passed quickly, and the dance was over sooner than I would have liked. Mary and I went our separate ways as the evening came to a close.

No sooner had the dance ended than I thought, "Well, that was big mistake. You had a great opportunity. Some guy is going to latch on to her before you ever see her again." Mary had told me that she worked at Ayres and I considered dropping in there and asking her out, but I didn't do that either. I eagerly awaited the following Sunday. To my dismay, she didn't attend the dance that evening. I was greatly disappointed. When would I have another chance to see her again? Well, it was my good fortune that opportunity arose at the next Sunday's dance. But that is another story, one that continued for more than 20 years.

Patricia Cupp

Patricia Cupp was born and raised in Indianapolis and graduated from Ball State University in 1964. After teaching English and Latin for 39 years, she is enjoying in retirement traveling, gardening, volunteering with writing projects and mentoring for School on Wheels.

She was born during WW II and marked its 50th anniversary with a trip to Normandy. She grew up in the prosperity of the 50s, through the Korean War and into the Cold War, and recently chalked up a 50th anniversary of graduation from high school. From 1968-70 she and her husband were Peace Corps volunteers in Ethiopia, and this past year she celebrated in Indianapolis with other returned volunteers the 50th anniversary of the founding of the Peace Corps. She concludes there's a lot to experience in half centuries.

Patricia assisted with this memoir project and volunteered in helping several other groups to complete their memoir projects.

My War Years

My mother, Ruby, married on her 18th birthday, three months before the bombing of Pearl Harbor. My father, half a year short of his twenty-first birthday, needed his mother to sign for the marriage certificate. Mother says she remembers as they climbed the old courthouse steps how uneven with wear they were and that my grandmother made a little joke about giving over her "little Dutch boy" as she had always called her sixth son, Joseph. My mother was marrying into the same family as her two older sisters, Mary and Virginia. My cousins would be "double" cousins and these two sets of aunts and uncles, my blood relatives times two.

My parents soon moved into the almost finished house my father had built, and they saved their money to furnish it bit by bit. I was born in November of the next year, and I was two months old when my father got his draft notice. I would not see him again for three years.

My father reported to Miami for basic training in the Army Air Force. My mom still has the souvenir booklet of photos Dad sent her showing the sightseeing boat he had taken on a cruise past famous homes and hotels along Miami Beach. He has written on the back of the booklet, "I will love you always." Officially now a GI Joe, he qualified as a tail gunner, but at 6'2" he was almost ten pounds over the weight limit. Instead, when he eventually shipped overseas, it was as a maintenance crew chief of a team assigned to Mustangs whose pilots did reconnaissance and escorted P-47s to their targets in the skies over Germany. In a small booklet stamped "passed by censor for mailing home," Mom was able to read on V-E Day the story of the bombing campaign by the XXIX Tactical Air Command. Later we would see photos of my father, long and lanky, leaning against airplanes, arms around *his* pilots. When he showed me the photos in which he is kneeling down with little Dutch and Belgian children, he liked to repeat a favorite joke: "No. Mommy, I don't want to go to the circus. I want to go watch the soldiers eat."

But all this I would only know later. The stories I was always told were of the years my mother lived with her older sister Loraine and how the two of them worked separate shifts and passed me between them. Mom worked the swing shift so it fell to Aunt Rene to give me dinner and a bath and put me to bed. So many times Aunt Rene told me how I always wanted to delay bedtime, how she would have to repeat as we climbed the stairs to my bedroom, "No more stories, no more songs." One evening she had been too tired to say anything, and she laughs remembering that I took her face between my hands and repeated the ritual words exactly as she had always said them. All my aunts staked a claim to me, but Aunt Rene's was the strongest. I had been delivered at my grandmother's home by the family doctor and Aunt Rene had bathed me in the kitchen sink and wrapped me in a blanket before taking me to my mother.

Mom and Aunt Rene often joked about the shortages of the war years. The lack of rubber meant my stroller clattered along on wooden wheels and the broken waist band of my underpants left them to drop about my ankles so often they thought I would never learn to walk. The picture Mother sent of the two of us to my father is my favorite still and treasured even more when Aunt Rene told me that was *her* best dress which Mother borrowed without permission because she thought the shoulder ruffles would photograph well. Aunt Rene had been so lonely for her husband she had sometimes gone to Union Station just to watch soldiers coming home on leave being greeted by loving families, even though she always ended up sitting on a bench crying a little.

After V-E Day my father had enough points finally to come home, while many in his outfit were issued tropical gear and boarded a troopship for the Pacific campaign. He was still stuck in France without transport home when the bombs were dropped on Japan, and its surrender meant his outfit made it home before he did. Mom and I moved back into our little house to await Dad's return and one day when Mom had dressed me up and ordered me to sit on the front step, a neighbor came by and asked me what the special occasion was. Though no such thing was true, without hesitation I informed her my father was coming home that day and she hurried away to tell everyone in the neighborhood the good news. Until then, my father had only been a photograph I always ran to get to show everyone. Though I very much became my father's daughter, when he did come home later that year and we went to Camp Atterbury to get him, they say I backed away when he tried to pick me up the first time.

     Years later a poetry exercise conjured up for me a puzzling set of images: a gray room upstairs where I was looking out the window and there was the smell of white shoe polish. When I mentioned it to my mom, she was astonished and told me something I had never heard before. Every night when she came home after midnight from her war job she had polished my little white shoes, washed the shoestrings, and put them on my bureau. Thus in the Working Women Hall of Fame there was Rosie the Riveter and there was my mom, Ruby, the Inspector of Dry Products at Eli Lilly, who polished my shoes every night. She was and is first among the many self-reliant women who raised me, whose love and care and courage made a secure world for me then and now. From it grew my oldest memory and the first poem I published which ends:

>   . . . . On the dresser
> white shoes smelling of polish,
> outside a branch brushing the screen,
> the moon and clouds move
> but I am still.
> It is warm where my knees touch,
> where I coil
> between shadow and dream
>
>   until now
> a rift in time
> brings this moment,
> pleasure of the eye looking
> at itself with everything around

moving, polished white.
It is only a small risk,
seeing what we were.

Third Grade

The great leveler of alphabetical seating placed Johnny Reardon in front of me in third grade. This was way too close to the class untouchable, bugger boy, as we called him. The only fortunate thing was I was spared the sight of his picking his nose and rolling the contents up and down his desk. My view was of his shaggy hair resting on a frayed collar of a once white shirt I was pretty sure had come from the church rummage sale, and downwind he smelled of my great aunt's closed house. He lived down the street from me so we walked to school each day in the same group, marshaled by our safety patrol person, the mighty Martin. Johnny was always last and no one asked him to hurry and catch up with us.

My mom had told me when he was five Johnny had been lost overnight and found in the morning asleep in the cemetery near our house. We seldom saw him playing in the yard of his tiny house where it was common knowledge a lot of drinking and playing of loud music often went on late into the night. Johnny was more likely to be ignored than teased, but one fall afternoon on the way home from school the neighborhood tough, Tommy Miles, started to taunt him.

"Hey, moron, I hear someone called the cops and your dad got arrested last night." Johnny walked slower and didn't look up. "Hey, I'm talking to you, snot."

We were almost to Johnny's when Tommy walked back to him. We all stopped and turned in morbid fascination as he punched Johnny roughly on the shoulder and Johnny ran toward his house. Tommy followed and just as they neared the driveway he knocked Johnny's books from under his arm and they flew into the water-filled ditch by the street.

What happened next may have been in part prompted by outrage at the bullying of the helpless, but far greater was my indignation at the sight of the brand new books we had been issued that year soaking in the muddy water. Something in me snapped. I dropped my books, charged, and head butted Tommy straight into the ditch. My friend said he sat there stunned, but I was already running madly for home and the safety of my mother's arms.

When I stopped sobbing and hiccupping, I told my mother what had happened and how I feared for my life when Tommy would catch up with me, to say nothing of the trouble I would be in when the safety patrol's report of my fighting was made to the principal. My mother, who had heard my jumbled reports before, why, for instance, a few years earlier my cousin and I had picked all of the unripe apples from our neighbor's tree and presented them in a small basket to him so he could make his apple cider early, listened silently. When I finished, I remember she kissed me on the cheek before she held me at arms' length for the lecture about how my fighting was wrong even though bullies needed to be confronted. She said I was right to stand up for Johnny, asked me to imagine a boy with no friends, and by dinner time I was feeling better about the whole thing.

My mom was called to school the next day and together we waited outside the principal's office. I studied Mom's face and tried to gauge what lay ahead. She was as pleasant looking as ever and she held my hand as we entered the principal's office. The two of them talked, I listened, and only once glanced up at my principal, the austere Mrs. Warner. Eventually I understood the long arm of the law had tapped me but then swept the incident aside, but I was warned further trouble would not be addressed in the same way. Back in class I was too contrite to appreciate the curious admiration of my classmates and took my place behind Johnny Reardon's empty seat.

By Christmas I had forgotten the Johnny Reardon incident. My friend Mary Beth and I each had Bobbsey Twins books to exchange and late on a cold afternoon just before the end of Christmas vacation I walked down the street to her house in my new Dale Evans cowgirl outfit and boots. It had started to sleet, but there was no way I was going to cover the grandeur of my fringed shirt and rawhide skirt with a winter coat.

Mother was horrified when she saw me slipping back into the house in my damp clothes and in two days the wisdom of her adage "Cold enters through the head and feet" was visited on me with a vengeance in the form of pneumonia. The doctor was summoned and I got my penicillin shot and spent the next week in bed. I missed the first week of school after vacation, and one afternoon when I was sipping lemon tea and reading *Lassie Come Home*, my mother came to tell me a friend, who missed me at school, had brought me a present. I assumed it was Mary Beth, but when she told me it was Johnny Reardon, I dropped the book of paper dolls he had brought in the exaggerated manner of all kids avoiding cooties. My mother frowned and reminded me my best friend had stopped by with homework assignments, but Johnny had brought me a gift. I could see her disappointment, and I went to sleep that night unable to shake the feeling I had fallen short and could, as my mother had said, be a better girl.

When word got out that Johnny Reardon had given me a present, I felt the full brunt of mean spirited teasing. "Hey, Patty, we hear Johnny Reardon's your boyfriend." With my new found fierceness I silenced this ugly accusation, but I let it be known there should be no more teasing of Johnny. Tommy Miles, who had always maintained I was a sneak who had caught him off guard, finally left me alone and no one else challenged me.

Next year Johnny was not in my class. Mary Beth and I graduated to Nancy Drew's and I actually got to ride a horse at the nearby stables. Jimmy Warner declared his affections for me by leaving a pearl necklace in our milk box one morning, and later we were married beneath the branches of the huge sycamore on the playground. Years later I look at the third grade group photo—me tall and at attention in the back row, Johnny seated with the other small ones on the front row. I remember being assigned Johnny as a spelling partner, pushing our desks together with our boxes of letters to be arranged correctly to practice the words on the week's spelling list. I made sure my letters never touched his despoiled desktop, but the day he passed his first spelling test with a C+, I had pried the gold star from my paper and put it on his. In the photo only Johnny looks down, not toward the camera.

Photographed Together on the Bridge He Built

     I remember my father's hands better than his face, his thick wrists and cracked nails, always a wound untended or scabbed over. He was the handsome workman finishing concrete or building a wall, breathing even with the labor. His hands around a trowel, the scoop and slap of mortar, his grunt with lifting blocks, stair stepping a foundation. His work clothes were so stiff with concrete and cement dust Mother washed them separately in the old wringer washer.
     When he started his construction business with his brother, I sometimes went to job sites with him on Saturdays. As he was flooring and framing a house, raising stairs and rafter beams, sawdust speckled his dark hair. I swept and practiced hitting a nail square to join scrap pieces of wood. I think of him when I hear the steady rhythm of roofing, a tap and single strike driving the nail home. Once he let me climb to the roof with him, his arms wrapped around me. He showed me his claw hammer and told me how one day he had started to slip from a steep roof, how he had driven it into the roof's wood, at the last minute breaking his fall. How he had laughed crazy, his feet hanging over the edge where his brother stood helpless below.
     It is my father's level I use, the one still rough from concrete residue, its viewing window spider cracked. When I heard it called a spirit level, I nodded, the magic properties in its gaseous green bubble confirmed. We had a competition, whose naked eye could gauge dead level better before the reading. I tilt my head the way he did, not hurrying the task. Check it again, he would say, and then the delicate adjustment.
     I take a deep breath and am carried back to the houses he built for our family, how mother had wanted marble window

sills for growing her plants and later walls removed to redefine the kitchen. And the dollhouse and the playhouse, the stilts he made for me, how he was so strong I could chin myself on his outstretched arm.

And any time I need a tool or wear blisters using it because I have removed my gloves, it is my father's prompting I remember, his pleasure in strength, his hand firm upon mine as it is in the photograph taken in autumn on the bridge he built long ago to the island in the small stream behind our house.

Belonging to the Day: Remembering Ethiopia

A small whirlwind gathers dust and dry grass in a haphazard rush across the open highland and disappears through the break in a crumbling wall. On the *ambas* of Ethiopia I have learned living is using stone: for stepping, walling, building churches, holding as weapons against stray dogs. On the town part of my hike to school I hear the clear drumming of mules, horses and donkeys on stone pavement. Already I have worn out the leather of my loafers and clomp softly along, a little taller, on soles retreaded at market with tire rubber.

I know just past the next leaning compound wall a small boy will emerge to ask the time. At the last possible moment he darts from the compound to plant himself in my path. He studies his toes and scratches his elbow until I am almost upon him. "*Sint seat new?*" he asks. I answer that it is the seventh hour of the day, but he frowns because I have not consulted a watch. He asks again why I do not have one and I shrug and point to the sun. The ritual complete, he shakes his head again at the foreigner who does not wear a watch she could obviously afford. He will ask again tomorrow.

More young children approach on their way back to afternoon school. "Good morning, class," the boldest one calls to me. What else can I answer to this unprecedented greeting? "Good morning, teacher," I say formally. She beams at me and runs giggling back to share the triumph of this exchange with her companions.

At the crest of the ridge I pause to gather myself for the descent. The land here drops sharply to the school below, then rolls gently to the first gorge two miles away. The Rift Valley stretches all the way to Kenya and the hydroelectric plant here provides our town of Debre Berhan with marginally reliable electricity. The historian Gibbon may have gotten the geography all wrong, but his description of this oldest independent nation in Africa is dead on: "Ethiopia . . . for a thousand years, forgetful of the world and by the world forgotten." But here I am, of the twentieth century, and I walk in and out of it every day. I teach how to teach English as a second language to secondary students who will teach in elementary schools. All this in a country already with dozens of languages, where the divine emperor who traces his line to Solomon and Sheba rules.

Rocks loosen with my climbing down the last steep part near the dorms of the Teacher Training Institute. I am met with the customary rush of greetings and questions from the girls who take from me the notebooks I have marked. "Miss, Miss, do you have the film for tonight?" "Miss, I am happy to be well and want to take my exam." "Miss Gunilla is looking for you." Gunilla, the Swedish volunteer and the only other woman on the staff, is my dearest friend. We will host a party for the students this evening to mark the end of the semester. When I enter my classroom everyone stands and the young men claim their notebooks. I administer semester exams and watch the dusty red birds outside my classroom. In the afternoon break I ask again of Ato Goshu, who is serving, "Why do we have tea in the morning and coffee in the afternoon?" He smiles blandly, as always. "Sugar?" he asks.

A final session, last minute questions and I gather the exams in my satchel. Somewhere in the Atlantic the wind is picking up to bring the short rains and we'll trade dust for mud and my way will be more difficult. I make the climb again, and just past the next *tukul* I feel a small hand in mine. There is Aleme, catching my stride and smiling shyly. I know each day she will join me at some point in my journey. She presses a small bouquet of purple flowers into my hand and one with too short a stem falls. "They're beautiful," I say. "What are they called?" "Purple flowers," she whispers and covers her mouth.

"*Ferengi*," a passing child calls out to me and Aleme lowers her head further. There is no hostility in this labeling me an "outsider," but I am always saddened by the forced separateness. Aleme and I walk on and I tease her by pulling the rain hat I have given her further down over her eyes. I ask if her baby brother is even fatter than when I saw him at the christening and she nods vigorously.

As the path turns we find ourselves sharing it with cows and goats and sheep being returned from the day's grazing. Our landlord's servant boy wields his stick furiously in an effort to bring some order to this bellowing procession. The herd's leader, whose silver hairs make her the grand lady who will enter our compound first, swings the gate open with a clatter of horns on sheet metal. The boy clouts the second cow in line to yield the right of way to us. I am home.

Frisco Gilchrist

Frisco Gilchrist grew up in Idaho. Burley was the town where his primary and secondary schooling took place. He reacts negatively when his bio reads "a native of Nebraska." Although family info and documentation confirm that he was born in Nebraska, he has no memory of a 'before Idaho.'

His life since Idaho, however, has been so varied in both time and place that he thinks of himself mostly as a world citizen. A first college degree was worked out in Oregon and Washington State. After serving as a mission-appointed pastor for a war-time Community Church in a housing project for the Puget Sound Naval Base, he studied sociology in Iowa, trained as an asylum attendant in New Jersey, taught in schools in Illinois and married a teacher there. In Tennessee he earned a Masters degree in Education, along with taking various overseas orientation courses. A mission assignment to Paraguay also provided a year of language study in Costa Rica.

Frisco lived and worked in Paraguay for 24 years and then put in 11 years as co-director of a denominational human rights program. Retired since 1977, he spent six months in Ontario, Canada and continues to travel the world as much and as often as possible.

Frisco

The name "Frisco" gets people's attention. Once new friends hear the "fr" sound as distinct from the "cr" and its image of vegetable shortening, they don't seem to forget my name. Outside the formalities of educational institutions, the "Sirs" and "Misters," and even the family name are easy enough to put aside, once it is realized that I respond best to simply "Frisco."

But there is, indeed, a story behind the name. It wasn't my father's idea, although I'm reasonably certain that he put the "F" initial in the middle of the name that went on my Nebraska birth certificate.

I grew up in Southern Idaho with only that initial as part of my name and went by my first name, "Marshall," which I never liked much. Later on, I realized that my dad and my uncles on the Gilchrist side also had middle initials rather than names. It must have been a family tradition. (My dad's initial "K" eventually became "Kay," by which he was known by most people throughout the latter half of his life.)

When in the mid 1940s I found myself in the role of teacher of children and adolescents in Central Illinois, one of my vivacious and admiring student friends decided that I must surely have a middle name that I was not owning up to and he took it upon himself to make me confess. He tried every name he could think of that started with an "f" and I denied each and every one. One day we were walking together when we had to wait for a freight train to go by. Several of the boxcars that went by had "FRISCO" painted in huge letters across their broad sides. They were the left-overs from an already dead railroad line with a name much too long to remember or pronounce (something like "St. Louis, Topeka, Santa Fe and San Francisco") that was made short by calling it the Frisco Line. While standing there watching "FRISCO" go by, it struck me that it wouldn't sound bad as a middle name; and, more importantly, at the moment it might be the way of stopping my young friend from hounding me about a middle name. So I said, "OK, if I have to have a middle name, that's it: Frisco." It worked. He and I found other things to talk about after that. Later on, I learned to say, "Yes, my name came from the side of a boxcar!"

But that's only the beginning of the story. It might have ended soon after and been forgotten if I hadn't found myself a few years later in San Jose, Costa Rica, concentrating on learning the Spanish language. When the Costa Ricans tried to pronounce "Marshall," it sounded like *macho* because their language doesn't use the "sh" sound, only the "ch." And on the streets of San Jose, in those days, stray donkeys wandered around looking for something to eat and were yelled at by the kids who liked to torment them with sticks and stones, shouting "*macho*! *macho*!" *Macho* is a much used and abused word in Spanish, meaning maleness, virility and male characteristics of all species, both admirable and vulgar. Only in Costa Rica, as far as I have discovered, was it applied specifically to donkeys. In any case, it hastened my decision to want to be known as "Frisco."

As we continued on south to Paraguay the following year, I was well aware that Paraguayans would have trouble with both my first and last names, since "Gilchrist" begins with a hard "G" followed by an "I" which also never happens in Spanish. So I cultivated "Frisco" from the beginning; and, since most of my work in the beginning was in a school where formality and respect had to be encouraged for the sake of discipline, I had to become "Mister Frisco." The Paraguayans bought into it immediately. It took many years for my dear wife to begin to call me "Frisco," but eventually she did. Sometimes she liked to complain that she married "Marshall," not "Frisco." Most of the in-laws still call me "Uncle Marshall." And my only brother and his family mostly avoid calling me anything at all but, without doubt, still find the "Frisco" signature strange.

Am I happy with it? You bet! It's who I am.

Spanked or Not?

In his declining years, my dad insisted several times on reminding me that in my childhood I had been such a good boy that I never needed to be spanked. My response was always that his memory must surely be playing tricks on him. I was unable, however, to come up with a convincingly clear memory of a real spanking.

My dad was, without a shadow of doubt, the disciplinarian in our family, and his standards were Scotch Presbyterian strict. He was never violent or brutal that I can recall. We were frequently disciplined verbally in no nonsense terms, but seldom touched.

Still, one memory is stuck in my mind of a time when I either received a spanking, felt so certain that I was going to get one that it seemed like I got it or felt so badly within myself for what had happened that it had the same effect as a spanking. I don't know which and am forced to conclude that I probably never will.

I must have been about eight years old. My brother Darwin was five years younger. During the first days of July, we had a few firecrackers and a small shaded farmhouse yard in which to explode them. There were no neighbors nearby, and our parents were often busy in the house or out at the barn. I had discovered that lighting the cracker under a tin can to blow it up into the air greatly increased the excitement. The two of us did it several times, being careful to get out of the way before it exploded. Then I wandered off to see or do something else—maybe to find the dog, who had retreated from the loud noises—and little brother attempted to blow a can into the air by himself. He didn't get out of the way soon enough. The can caught him in one eye in such a way that it effectively destroyed the eyeball. That accident destined him to a lifetime with one glass eye.

But the "spanking" came the next day. After the emergency trip to the hospital and the other necessary adjustments to the situation, I was commissioned—as a mild punishment for my inattentiveness the day before, I think—to clean up the yard. Every tin can, fireworks scrap, stick and stone was to be disposed of. But I didn't do it. And after a reasonable lapse of time, I still hadn't done it. That was spanking time—or should have been!

Earliest Memory

Sometimes I'm in a quandary as to whether I actually remember a detail of my early life or only have a memory picture of it because of photographs I've seen and stories I've heard that make me feel like it's a memory. The latter is the case of the journey with my parents from Nebraska to Idaho in my dad's carpenter-built truck-house.

I would like to think that something of that journey is my own memory, but I know it's not. The picture of me—my parents' firstborn—standing in the doorway of that truck-house like a royal prince of some kind, fascinates me. That picture was my single request when my younger sister, many years later, offered me the opportunity to claim any items from the old family album before she passed it on to her daughters. I have imagined what that mostly wooden "house" on wheels might have looked like on the inside and what kind of westward travel experience it would have provided. No doubt short on creature comforts and space, it would have been equipped with well-shaved and sanded cabinets and storage bins to keep our meager possessions and supplies in order. My carpenter dad would have seen to that. I shudder to think of what kind of stove it may have had for heat and cooking, but I know it had a stove-pipe chimney. I've seen the stove-pipe in pictures, but all the rest is in my imagination. I don't remember any of it. Stuck in my mind is the fact that the traveling house was built on a "Rio" truck chassis, but that's because Dad would occasionally, with pride, talk about it after I was mature enough to understand what he meant.

When I was a young teenager, I also made the discovery that our family was already friends with a family in Sheridan, Wyoming, which had to mean that we shared time and experience with them on that original trip west. But while I remember the later visit with them in Wyoming, I have no memory of how we originally became acquainted with that family.

Without question, however, I feel able to identify the moment which is my earliest childhood memory. I must have been about four years old. The unchanging place/scene in my memory consists of the top landing of a stairway—leading into a room or maybe just a hallway—of some residential building of some kind, somewhere in Idaho and a travel trunk with three sorrowful people (my father, my mother and me) kneeling beside it to pray. The news that my dad had just delivered was that my younger brother, Eldon, had died. He was 20 months of age. My mother later confirmed for me that it was Steptocci Laryngitis that killed him. (My mind tells me that we probably didn't—or couldn't—get him to a doctor soon enough.) That must have been my major introduction to the hardships and disappointments of life. I think that's why I remember it.

The Violin

There must be a human story in the fact that two violins have spent some 55 years together in a trunk at Anibal Fadlala's house in Asuncion, Paraguay. During those years I have tried various times to imagine what that story might be. Is it about the strength and weakness of a friendship between two men who had only a few common interests? Or is it about how musical instruments depend upon humans to keep them alive by playing them? Maybe it's about music itself which longs to be created and feels rejected by those who could have made more of their opportunity. Or, if it's none of the above, I still think there must be the makings of a good story in that trunk.

In the Burley, Idaho, High School Orchestra days, I was pretty good on the violin and took pride in receiving excellent ratings at the Idaho State Music Festivals. Some private lessons in the beginning and my mother's insistence that I practice regularly was paying off in satisfactions and led to my dad's willingness to invest in a better instrument when I needed it.

Neglect started as soon as I went to college. The violin went with me, but it didn't get to make much music as my time and energies were absorbed in other pursuits. When it arrived with me in San Jose, Costa Rica, I was totally neglectful of it while all my energies went into learning the Spanish language. Then one day I noticed that some mold was growing on it. I thought that a little direct sunlight would take care of the mold and placed the violin on the patio where the morning sun could do its thing. But I forgot and left it in the sun too long, and when I went to retrieve it before the afternoon rain, I found that a bit of glue that held the back panels together had also melted in the sunlight, causing a crack in the sound box.

The now-cracked violin continued our journey south to the tiny (by South American standards) country of Paraguay. It was introduced to some fifth and sixth grade music classes in the school I was assigned to, despite its not greatly noticeable tone defect. Then it was retired from all active duty.

Meantime, I had become acquainted with Anibal, a businessman and graduate of the school, who was happy to take care of money exchanges and other business matters for me and to practice his English on me while I practiced my Spanish on him. One day he told me that he, too, had played the violin in his youth and that his instrument also needed some repair. He thought he knew an artisan in a nearby rural town who could repair both violins for us. So my violin joined his to go to the country. I never saw it again nor heard details about its experience. When I finally remembered to inquire, I was told that the artisan found that he could not repair the violins and that they were both resting in a trunk at Anibal's house.

Over the following years, I have asked from time to time if anything ever developed in regard to their possible repair, but the answer was always the same: they are together in the trunk. There is never a suggestion that I should reclaim mine, and since I know its usefulness to me is long since gone, I figure that it cannot be any more unhappy where it is than it would be with me!

That's the violin's story. I'd still like to discover the human story.

Meeting Jedd

He is probably the best friend I could have hoped to find after moving to downtown Indianapolis five years ago. He's much younger than I—by nearly 40 years. And he is a contrast to me in a number of ways because our life experiences have been so different. Still, we have a lot in common: a love for music—especially the Indianapolis Symphony and good organ music—, an appreciation for good theatre—especially the smaller theatres of the Mass Ave district—and a fascination with and concern for our fellow human beings. We like each other's company, both when we want to talk and when we fall into silence. We learn to appreciate life more by listening to each other's perspectives. I like to say, "We're good for each other." We both have questioning and impatient minds—especially about Christianity and religions in general. We attend different churches, however. Seriously ask either one of us about how we became acquainted and you will hear that we believe there was an element of divine guidance to our coming together.

My dear wife died in March of 2006 after 56 years of married companionship. I wanted to leave the apartment in the retirement center where we had lived the many years of her disability, after a stroke immobilized her right side (but not her mind, thank God!). The new owners of that retirement community were not willing to allow me to move to a smaller apartment. I also wanted to stop driving and being responsible for the upkeep of an automobile. So I looked for an apartment downtown ("where the action is!"). A couple who had been our friends for years now lived downtown in their retirement, so I felt safe and able to keep some familiar contacts. They were also active members of a book-study group that met every other Wednesday morning to discuss the latest writings of scholars who study the origins of the Bible and other religious literature. I had known about the group but never felt free to leave my wife to go across town to a book club. Now I could and had an easy ride from downtown.

Within weeks of my joining the book group, a few of us made an overnight trip to Northern Indiana to hear lectures by a couple of the authors we had been reading. One of the fellows with whom I rode that weekend, proud of the progressiveness of his suburban church near Indianapolis, urged me to visit that church. I was willing, but complained that I would need help to get there, since I had already sold our vehicle. That needn't be a problem, I was told, because a young man who attends their services lives near downtown and would be glad to pick me up some Sunday. He gave me a name and a telephone number, and I made the contact and arranged a date that would be convenient for both of us.

Although I sat through the worship service that Sunday with the man who had invited me and thought well of the sermon we heard, I found myself much more interested in the conversations we had getting there and returning. My driver seemed unusually open-minded, frank and honest. He was not only friendly, but somehow inspired my trust. I wanted to see him again. So, when a week or two later I was wanting someone to attend a symphony concert with me, I thought of him. When I called to ask him, his positive response seemed enthusiastic. Our exploration of each other's likes and dislikes had begun.

Oh, yes! In addition to our common interests mentioned at the beginning of this tale, we soon agreed that we liked to travel and acquaint ourselves with the rest of the world. While my health lasts and our bank accounts hold up, and whenever he accumulates enough vacation days from the computer where he works to "adjudicate" the merits of applications for disability assistance, we head for another part of the planet. (We've been to Scotland, to Paraguay and Brazil and to Spain already.) Jedd is a God-send for me, whose age plus sometimes serious balance problems make it unwise to travel alone.

Beverly L. Harrington

As a child, Beverly was not very outspoken and often allowed herself to be overlooked. The seventh child in a house of eight children, she found it difficult to be heard above the crowd. The death of her father when she was a young child left a void in her life that was never filled. The feeling that no one was interested in what she had to say was the seed that started her to write. The earliest encouragement to take her writing seriously was from her eighth grade English teacher.

Beverly has two sons, six healthy grandchildren and six great-grandchildren. Retired from nursing, she now has the time to work on her hobbies. She often balances her oil painting and writing alongside of cake decorating. In times of great depression, her use of pen and paper has proven to be the door that lets the sun shine through.

As an individual who takes great joy in learning new things, Beverly used to work on cars with her husband, Ollie. Years later, this proved to be beneficial when she went car shopping alone. Of the many subjects that interest her, though, the human body is the one topic that, to this day, will cause her to stop everything, sit down and start to study like a schoolgirl.

The Red Slippers

I was four years old when my father passed away, so my mother was the only rule maker in the family and she raised the eight of us alone. Mother stood five feet, five inches. But, when I was in trouble, she appeared to be six feet tall. Most of the time just a look from her and I would get the message. As a parent, she demanded discipline and dealt with us if we disobeyed. No, my mother was not abusive, but if she sent me out for a switch, it had better be one that lasted through my punishment. I always felt she was particularly hard on her three girls. She always said, "I want you girls to be able to take care of yourselves if you ever have to."

Someone gave my mother a pair of apple-red slippers that were brand new, still in the box. The size was a seven and my older sister and I were allowed to see who could fit the slippers. My sister put the slippers on and paraded around until her feet began to hurt and she started to limp. I forced my feet in them and Mother could see right away they were too small. To avoid a fight over the slippers, Mother put them away, with the firm instruction to keep our hands off. It would be a month before she could buy another pair of slippers so the two of us would each have a pair. My sister put her claim on the slippers even though we were forbidden to touch them.

The weather outside was beginning to turn cold, but daytime still held a little warmth. For weeks I had begged my mother to let me go to the Veterans Day Parade. School was out and I made sure my housework was completed. Before Mother went to work that morning, she said, "Okay, you can go." While my sister was on the telephone, I tucked the slippers under my coat and quickly left the house. I went to my best friend's house and changed into the slippers. My feet felt comfortable and warm so off we went to the parade. The slippers made my skinny legs look so grown up. As the day moved on, my legs grew cold because the temperature began to drop. By noon, the bottom of my feet began to burn and my pinched toes were numb. Despite all of this pain, I had to walk wherever we went. I had pain if I stood still or if I moved. I was cold and I hurt all over my body from the tightness of those shoes. After the parade was over, my friend and I walked a little deeper into town to the baker. Because I used my bus fare to buy Mexican wedding ring cookies, we had to walk home for a total of 13 blocks.

Through what seemed like a lifetime of pain, I reached my house almost at a run. As I reached for the door knob, I could hear my mother's voice inside. I froze in my tracks because I had the slippers on my frozen, aching feet. I put my body in reverse to walk three additional blocks to my best friend's house. One half hour later, I walked back to my house where my mother asked about the parade with all its floats and bands. I told her as much as I could recall through the pain. When she was not looking, I put the slippers back where she had placed them, never wanting to see them again. I never told my mother what I did because I felt I had punished my own self that day. I do not know what happened to the slippers and I truly do not care. At present, I have three pairs of red shoes, but I don't think that I have worn any one pair even five times. My mother could not have created a punishment to top the one I gave myself.

The Fall of the Bully

The position of bully was a temporary one at best in my childhood neighborhood. The Flanner House playground, formerly located on the corner of 16th Street and Missouri Street, was where we went to play in the neighborhood. A multipurpose center, the Flanner House served as a daycare, an afterschool gathering place and an adult education facility. During the day, there were the happy sounds of children throughout the one-story building. However, as evening approached, there was the noise of equipment in the cannery and saw mill and, at the other end of the property, women were being instructed on the use of sewing machines. The center was closed on the weekend, and this was when the children of the area claimed the playground.

For both toddlers and teens, this small, dusty patch of rough land was a haven to burn off the energy that dwelled in each of us. The playground was not enclosed by a fence so we had free access to the grounds. Three sets of swings and two sliding boards occupied the east end of the unpaved grounds. Here the older sister and brothers looked after their younger siblings at play. South of the two slides stood a pole with one end encased in concrete and the other end rising high in the air and supporting a large board. Someone had nailed the rim of a broken bushel basket to the board. This was the basketball court. As the older boys passed the ball to one another, dense brown dust filled the air. Orders of "Pass it to me," or "Get the ball, man," were yelled from one team member to another. Last of all, in the southwest sector of the grounds, stood a well-used baseball screen with its two poles encased in concrete. This was the baseball diamond, with bases made of wood slabs covered by mud after a heavy rain. The pitcher's mound was a brick in the middle of the diamond. The only concrete walkway was painted for a game of hopscotch with a rock.

On one hot July Saturday afternoon the playground was filled with action. Walking onto the playground, tossing his baseball in the air, Freddy yelled, "Who wants to play baseball?" He was a tall boy with large hands who looked older than his true age. From every corner of the playground, stampeding children of all sizes, with their hands waving, shouted, "Me, pick me!" It was an unwritten rule that the owner of the baseball was the captain of the first team. The second captain was a self-appointed big bully by the name of Duncan. Duncan, whose family was somewhat new to the area, did not pose a threat to boys his size or older. But it was not unusual to see him grab smaller kids by the collar with his fist hovering over their head. "I am second captain," yelled Duncan as he pushed his way through the crowd. Right away, the team players were picked from the dusty brown hands waving in the air. At the end of the selection, the team under Duncan was one player short. Duncan began to feel he was cheated out of the good players because everyone had wanted to play for Freddy.

One skinny boy who had been passed over continued to plead to be selected to play. The boy's name was Willie, and he had a handicapped arm. Willie's left arm and hand were normal; however, his right arm stopped at the elbow, with little, undeveloped fingers on the end of it. Jumping up and down, waving his good arm, Willie continued to call out, "I'll play for you, Duncan, pick me. I will play for you," as the tears ran down his dusty brown cheeks. The angry Duncan pushed the smaller boy aside like a rag doll and he fell to the ground. Standing over the crying boy with both of his fists clenched, Duncan yelled, "You are a cripple and you can't play no ball."

From out of nowhere came a girl with a facial expression that made the crowd of other players part. With her two fists clenched and her bottom lip tucked in her mouth, in one forceful leap, she jumped on Duncan's back and sent him to the ground, face first. The call, "fight, fight, fight" rang out all over the playground, and like bees, other children swarmed to see the fight. In dust and dirt was Dee, Willie's older sister, beating the bigger boy about the head and face. As she used every muscle to keep the bigger boy down, her little brother joined in the fight. Kicking Duncan in the side and hitting him with his one good hand, Willie forgot his fear of this giant.

Pushing Dee off of his back, Duncan managed to get to his knees and notice that his nose and face were bleeding. Once more, he pushed Willie aside, but this time he began to run. A group of children followed, laughing as they went. After dusting herself off and consoling her brother, Dee began her walk home.

As for the baseball game, well, it was called off due to no second team and one good fight.

Strangers in the Night

When I was seventeen, I took a trip to Maine to visit a high school classmate. A year after graduation, she had married a Marine who was stationed at the Portsmouth Naval Shipyard. The shipyard is on an island located in Kittery, Maine, with a mailing address of Portsmouth, New Hampshire. This trip, as it turned out, offered a host of firsts for me. But some of the events gave me the strange feeling that I had been in the same situation before. To begin with, I had never been on a plane before this trip. The flight from Indianapolis was wonderful; however, on the second leg of the trip, the flight was turbulent and bumpy. Another first was that once I landed I met a shy freckle faced young man. This tall stranger of slim build appeared to be someone I had met before. I felt that I had done all of this before this night.

The young man was named Ollie, and he was a Marine stationed at the same military base as my friend's husband. My classmate Charlie and I were so excited to see one another I hardly noticed the young man riding in the front seat. Charlie and I giggled and chattered about old times and the latest gossip as we rode back to the base housing from the airport, a trip that took one and a half hours. As we let Ollie out of the car later that evening, I noticed he had a face full of freckles. It was another first for me; I had never seen a black man with freckles.

The next day turned out to be very warm so the four of us went to the beach. This, too, was a first because I had never seen the ocean. Ollie and I took our shoes off to walk in the water. Its frigid temperature went with jet speed to my brain. I was out of the water right away, but Ollie tried to save face and remain there. I could see he was cold because he became very pale and smoked three cigarettes to try to keep warm. Once he got warm, he began to talk and open up about himself. He talked about how one day he and his childhood friend had planned to join the Marine Corps together, but the next morning his friend did not meet him at the recruitment office. Thinking his friend would come later, Ollie carried out his part of the plan. As it turned out, his friend never did enlist and was just joking the day before. The one fear that Ollie spoke of was the possibility of going to fight in the Vietnam War, like so many of his friends. The weekend was packed with fun and discoveries for the two of us. The ocean, we discovered, had a soothing effect on us as we became better acquainted.

At the end of the weekend, Ollie asked if I would return for a second time, if he sent me a ticket in two weeks. I said, "maybe," but I had no question in my mind that my mother was not going to say yes to another trip so soon. Charlie and her husband teased me about coming all the way to Maine to find a sweetheart. My concern was not my mother's objection as much as it was my personal worry. I was a college student and already engaged to a young man in the Air Force. However, while stationed in France, my Airman had forgotten to write for five months so I wrote my first and only "Dear John" letter. After three months of my flying to and from Maine, Ollie and I were married in New Hampshire.

Our marriage lasted for 22 years and we were blessed with two sons. One of the great things about our marriage was that we would sometimes do things on impulse. Yes, we planned most of our normal activities, but every once in awhile, we put the boys in the car and took a weekend trip without a plan. We were both kids when we married and so in a way we grew up together. Ollie passed away in 2009. As it turned out, the shy stranger with freckles who refused to admit to cold feet in the water will never be forgotten.

Linda Shaw

Linda spent her childhood on a cattle farm in the flat prairies of Illinois, plodding along barefoot on dusty cow paths, hunting baby kittens in the hayloft and riding her bicycle. She received an AB in English from Illinois College and an MSL at age 45 from Indiana University.

After college she lived in Boston, attempted to teach English in the inner-city schools of Chicago, married an advertising executive and gave birth to two daughters, Heather and Holly. After an unsuccessful year as a middle school librarian, she finally found her true career as a librarian at the University of Indianapolis.

Linda has always loved to read and write. She is a Master Gardener and an environmentalist, and her current passions are ballroom dancing, classical music and genealogy.

Barns

No one in the 1940s had a swing set in their backyard—at least not in our neck of the woods that was rural Central Illinois. No swing sets, no TV, no little leagues, but we had something much better—we had barns. No two barns were alike. Each had its own flavor, its own unique character.

The Kunken's barn smelled of old milk mixed with hay and manure because they milked about six to eight cows every day. I well remember perching on a milk stool, shivering in the January cold, while I watched Helen Margaret milk her two cows at 6 a.m. Their barn had a large hayloft with high ceilings. Way up on the west end of the hayloft there was a very high slatted platform positioned almost to the roof. To reach it we had to climb a rough ladder of planks that had been nailed to the studs sticking out from the wall. We took great delight in sitting up there and scaring ourselves silly by looking through the slats to the floor far, far below.

The Banister's barn had a staircase to reach the hayloft. One hot summer we discovered that the bales of hay were stacked high on each side of the hayloft and hanging down from the center of the roof was a thick rope with a huge, gnarly knot at the end. We could snag the rope, climb to the top of one stack of bales, sit on the knot and swing all the way across the haymow to the stack of bales on the other side. It was exhilarating and as scary as any ol' carnival ride since we whizzed high above the opening to the ground floor where the stairs were. We had great fun that summer until the day Joyce Kunken let go. We were aghast! How could she have done that? Luckily she didn't fall all the way to the ground floor of the barn. She landed on the top two or three staircase steps. But she did hurt herself—she had sprained an ankle and Mr. Banister laid down the law: "No more playing in our barn!" I was exceedingly peeved for a long time at Joyce Kunken for letting go of that rope. What a wimp! There was no reason to let go. The knot to sit on was big. All you had to do was hang on.

Unfortunately, there was never a convenient rope hanging in my own barn—nor was there any high platform to test our fortitude. Our barn was red with white stripes. It had a hay-strewn corridor running through it, from front to back. On the left was an oats bin that was fun to jump around in when the oats were fresh. Later—not so much—the barn cats considered it their litter box. After the oats bin were two stalls for the milk cows and two stalls for Dan and Don, the work horses. The mangers had hay in them and a feedbox for grain at either end. Halfway down the corridor was a ladder to the haymow. To the right, were more stalls, sometimes used to store equipment, to shelter new calves or to doctor a sick animal.

The barn smelled of old manure and past harvests of oats and hay. It was quiet and peaceful; at times the only sound was the flutter of the barn swallows as they whipped to and from their mud nests on the east wall. Other times, you could hear the cows and horses munching their dinner or restlessly moving their feet, flicking the flies with their tails.

On various spring days my mom would say to me, "I think if you look, you might find some baby kittens in the barn." Off I would go to search the barn from top to bottom. The mama cats seemed to favor the mangers, and I would sometimes find a litter of newborn kittens living right under the nose of the milk cow. The litters were fairly easy to find if the cats bedded down in the mangers. Searching in the hayloft was a different matter. If high stacks of hay bales were still in the loft, then it was a challenge to find the kittens, as there were all sorts of hidey holes that cats could wiggle into. However, find them I did, and then I watched and waited impatiently until the kittens were old enough for me to play with. Sometimes the mother cats had enough of me and would move their kittens, and so I would have to search all over again. There were a couple of shallow pans in the corridor that Daddy would fill with warm, steaming milk for the cats. If I were in the barn with him when he was milking, he would amuse me by squirting milk directly from the cow's teats into the mouths of the cats.

I tamed scores of kittens. Not many had long lives for we didn't call the vet for our pets. Distemper would kill them and feral tomcats liked to kill kittens. Then, there was

DDT. Not knowing how lethal it was, my Dad sprayed all surfaces in the barn, and that wiped out our entire family of cats. I have never forgotten seeing Spitfire, a gold striped feral tomcat, twitching, shaking and dying on the floor of the horse stall. We had to get a new family of cats from neighbors, and after that, Daddy was careful to only spray the walls in the barn.

I loved the haymow. I liked to climb on the prickly bales of hay and create forts with them. There was a small window/door that looked toward the house, and when I was playing my imaginary cowboys and Indians, it served as a lookout post. When the loft was empty, the floor—rubbed smooth and shiny from years of dragging bales across it—was fun to slide on.

It's gone now. The barn is gone. My grandmother built it and the house in 1918. Over the years the prevailing west winds had caused the barn to lean eastward, and so in the 40s my dad had a concrete brace poured along the east foundation. When my dad died in 1968, there were no more farm animals in the barn. Little by little, it fell into disrepair. In the 80s straight line winds pushed it ever further to the east and it finally collapsed sideways. My brother-in-law sold the barn to scavengers for the old wood planks and they finally took it completely away a few years ago. To look at the house now, with no barn behind it, is like looking at a picture puzzle of the Mona Lisa with the puzzle piece over her mouth missing.

Going Back in Time

On a hilltop overlooking flat, Illinois farmlands and bordered on the south by meandering Salt Creek, there lies a small graveyard called Pleasant Valley Cemetery. It has also been called the Warren Cemetery by some, as it was carved from the homestead of Uriah and Sarah Warren who migrated there in 1845 from Pike County, Ohio, and the majority of the people sleeping there are descended from, or related to, the Warrens.

As a child growing up about six miles from this cemetery, I visited there occasionally with my parents. My father's mother was a daughter of Uriah and Sarah Warren. Daddy pointed out to me his mother's grave and the graves of her young siblings who did not live to 1937 as Nellie did, but were taken in September, 1873, by a cholera epidemic that devastated the Warren family. The story is told that in the late summer of that year two men from a flatboat on Salt Creek were ill and taken in to be nursed by the Warren family. By the end of September, the family patriarch, Uriah, was dead, as was his wife's brother, James, and her father, Hugh Johnson, who was 83 years old. Six year old Sarah and 12 year old Perry were also stricken and died. Edgar, who was 19 and had his bags packed to go to Lincoln College, passed away on September 7th. It is said that his gold coins were buried with him. Uriah's brother, Lemuel, died on August 28th, his wife soon after, and their son-in-law, Patrick Gallagher, also died.

The cemetery was a peaceful place, set back from the country road by perhaps a quarter of a mile. I remember my teacher, Russell Morris, taking the 5th and 6th grade students on a hike down the railroad tracks, across the railroad trestle bridge and up through the cemetery where he showed us his parents' graves. We lingered in the quiet of the cemetery for perhaps a half hour, resting and playing among the gravestones, sometimes stopping to decipher the inscription on a child's stone watched over by a chubby cherub.

On September 11, 2010, at the invitation of the Knapp/Chesnut/Becker Library Museum in Middletown, I returned to the cemetery to participate in a cemetery walk. I dressed in a period costume and chose to portray my great-grandmother, Sarah Warren. As I stood at her grave, telling her story, I could see across the fields to the stately two story home that she and Uriah had built. Nothing had changed in those 60 years since I had been to the cemetery as a child. Yet everything had changed. Now my parents' graves are there and my favorite teacher, Mr. Morris, lies next to the graves he pointed out to us.

It was an interesting day because I met at least three cousins I didn't know existed and learned that almost everyone in that cemetery has some connection to the Warren family. I brought with me my father's highchair from 1896 and placed it on his grave. On the highchair I placed a copy of a memoir I had written about my father. I could have chosen to portray either of my parents but felt that the connection was too close and that I would find it difficult to speak about them. I was pleased that some took the time to read my father's story.

As I browse through a roster of those interred at Pleasant Valley Cemetery, looking at birth dates and death dates and searching for connections, I find myself wishing that those ancestors had written their memoirs and left them for me. Would that I knew all of the stories that those stones represent.

Hide and Seek

For the most part, I was a pretty good kid. I always did my homework and made good grades, obeyed my parents, got my 4-H projects done on time, did almost everything that was expected of me. However, once in a while, I pushed the envelope—although we didn't use that expression in 1956 when I was a junior at Middletown High School.

Our little school of 40 students always produced a junior play and a senior play. These were money-makers for the class treasury, and we always had a good turnout for our productions. My class put on *A Feudin' Over Yonder* in our junior year, and it went over so well, that we produced *Hillbilly Weddin'* the next year.

I loved being in plays. I usually got the lead since I was a loud mouth and the audience could hear me. The part I loved most about being in plays, however, was getting to be with my friends backstage during all the rehearsals and being near whatever boy was the current object of my desire. My diary is peppered with expressions and comments. If I were "real gone" on someone I would describe him as "a living doll" and record, "He is a darling—the most—he sends me—absolutely." If the living doll held hands with another girl then . . . "Honestly—I could bawl," I would write in my diary.

The other perk to being in plays was getting to drive the family car the five miles to town for play practice in the evening. After play practice, those of us who had cars would drive around Middletown. Middletown had a population of 500 folks. There were two main streets that ran the length of the town, north and south, plus a couple of other shorter north/south streets with many cross streets and a few alleys. The town had no stoplights and only a few stop signs. If there were streetlights, I don't remember them. By the time we got out of play practice there was no traffic at all on the streets.

At first, we just crammed our friends in our cars and drove around town. Then we started playing hide and seek with the cars, eventually driving around with the headlights off. This pastime began in March, 1956, when I was a sophomore and had a part in the FHA/FFA play the home economics teacher was producing.

On Monday, March 19, I wrote in my diary:

We had play practice tonight. Ronnie had the car. So did I— that is—after I took Daddy to the Legion meeting. After play practice I was driving around & Ronnie followed me. We really tore up & down those streets. Then he got ahead of me & I lost them & couldn't keep up with them turning corners that fast. They pulled up alongside of me once & asked what happened to me? I don't know where they went to. I couldn't find them. Kenneth was with Ronnie. I'll have to ask them where they went.

I would have been driving our turquoise and white 1955 Ford Fairlane with the fancy dip in the chrome on the front doors. My classmate, Ronnie, would have been driving the Janssen's blue, 1955 Chevrolet. These were big cars, very long and wide when compared to today's automobiles.

I am amazed that I dared to do all that driving around while Daddy was in town at the Legion Hall! I was 15 and Ronnie was also 15. We did not have driver's licenses.

The next school year when we were going to rehearsals for *A Feudin' Over Yonder*, we again had a gay old time every night after play practice. We zipped up and down the streets of Middletown trying to ditch each other. We would turn our lights out and sneak around trying to hide. We had a blast!

Opening night, which was also closing night, was drawing near. We were in the last week of rehearsals. On Tuesday morning, when my alarm went off, all of a sudden I was startled to see my dad walk into my bedroom. My heart sank. Daddy never came into my bedroom.

"Where did you go last night?" he demanded.

"Uhhh, to play practice," I timidly offered.

"There are 20 extra miles on the odometer," he said. "Where did you go?"

"Uh, uh . . . nowhere," I stuttered.

"Where did you go?" he asked in a slightly louder voice.

"Ummm, uh . . . I drove around town a little," I ventured.

"Well," he said, "there will be no more driving to play practice for you. You can still be in the play. I don't want to disappoint the others, but you won't be driving the car into town anymore! Rose Ellen will drive you to play practice."

So that was the end of car hide and seek for me. Obviously, some townsperson had tipped my father off as to what was going on, and he checked the mileage on me. The play was a success, and since I usually only needed to be told once, I soon was behind the wheel of the Ford Fairlane again.

"Where the Boys Are"

According to the film critic, Robert Horton, "The movie that put the 'break' into 'spring,' *Where the Boys Are,* inspired thousands of college kids to seek sun, surf and even s-e-x on the beaches of Florida." In this 1960 film, a crowd of co-eds heads to Fort Lauderdale to find amusement, as well as romance. "It's a dressier, glossed-up version of the 'Problems with Today's Youth' movies that were filling up the drive-ins of the era," Horton writes. The cast includes Yvette Mimieux, Paula Prentiss, Jim Hortan and Connie Francis. It's Francis who sings the delightful title song in which she declares that "in the crowd of a million" she will find her "valentine."

Product Description
A group of Midwest girls head down to Ft. Lauderdale, Florida for spring break.

That was us—Barge, Char, Marilynn and I—four college girls from a Midwest school, Illinois College, heading down to Ft. Lauderdale for spring break. I can't remember when I saw the movie. I don't remember who had the idea that we should go to Florida on spring break. It was probably Barge or Marilynn who were big city girls from Detroit and Chicago. Char and I were Central Illinois farm girls. I'm almost certain that my parents did not see this movie that came out the year before our trip. Had they seen the movie, I doubt that I would have a story to tell.

Sat. Feb. 25, 1961
Dear Folks,
You are now reading a letter from one of the luckiest girls there ever was. The most exciting thing has just happened. Marilynn's former boyfriend (now her boyfriend) Jimmy who is a jet pilot in the navy drove up this weekend in his 1960 Pontiac from Florida and guess what—he is leaving his car here for a month so we can drive it to Florida

Spring vacation! He wants Marilynn to come and see him then and that is how lucky us will get to Florida. . . .

March 2, 1961
Dear Folks,
 Well, only 3 weeks and one day until spring vacation . . . We have been doing exercises every night so as to be in "good shape" by Florida time. I am very stiff and sore from them. I walk around like an old woman.

March 17, 1961
Dear Folks,
 Well, only one more week. I don't know what we're going to do when the time finally does get here—we're so excited now we can hardly contain ourselves.

 Friday, March 24, 1961 finally arrived. After we all ate lunch in Baxter Hall, we piled into Jimmy Crump's car and began our drive straight through to Florida. We adhered strictly to a rotation plan for drivers and co-pilots. After driving for two hours, one was rewarded with two hours of sleep in the back seat. Then it was back to the front passenger seat to be co-pilot which meant you had to stay awake and keep the driver alert and headed in the right direction. After a session as co-pilot, you once again got a two hour nap in the back before it was your turn to drive again. It actually worked very efficiently. We drove through the night, and I still remember my joy when the sun came up the next morning, revealing a marvelous green world. We had left behind all things dreary, grey and leafless. In the South things were green! It was like a miracle to me who had never been south in the winter before. Seeing the verdant landscape and blooming dogwoods seemed to be a heralding of all good things yet to be experienced on this trip.
 We arrived at the airbase near Jacksonville, Florida, at 10 a.m. on Saturday and delivered Jimmy's car to him. We stayed overnight and Jimmy took us to eat at the Bachelor Officers' Quarters. On Sunday, he drove us to Fort Lauderdale, and we found a place to stay just one block from the beach

and perhaps two blocks from the Elbow Room. For a bedroom, living room, kitchen and bathroom, the four of us paid $25 a day. Total! I complained that that was more than we had planned to pay. Then for the next seven days and nights, it was party, party, party.

During the day we would go to the beach with the other 35,000 college students and ogle each other. At night we went to the bars. The drinking age in Florida was 21, but we had all obtained new driver's licenses from the Illinois Bureau of Motor Vehicles and a skilled fellow on campus had altered our "lost" ones to put each of us over 21. We were a little worried for Char as hers said she was 28, but she was only questioned about it once. Our favorite hang-out was the Elbow Room, and our favorite drink was beer. If you wanted a boy to buy you a drink, you had to drink beer. That is when I learned to drink beer.

Every night we flirted and talked to lots of boys from schools all over the South, the Midwest and the East Coast. Each night I had a new boyfriend with whom I would walk on the beach and smooch. No sex, though. No one in our group was into casual sex. Other than drinking too much, we acted fairly decent. I do remember a young man named Jerry Meyers from Mobile, Alabama. I think I hung out with him two nights. At one point he and I were walking in a residential area and spotted a coconut on a tree that was not too tall. I climbed on his shoulders and was able to reach the coconut. I tugged and tugged and all of a sudden, it came loose, hit me on my head, bounced off of his head and fell to the ground. In the distance I heard someone laughing at us. I brought that coconut home and had it in my dorm room for a long time.

On one of the nights, we had a riot. One young man decided to climb the traffic light that hung over A1A, just outside the Elbow Room. He began to lead college cheers and songs, and the police began trying to get him down. The bars emptied. A1A filled up with college kids. Policemen surrounded the bottom of the pole, waiting for him to come down. My friends and I were in the midst of the melee, laughing and singing and shouting. Marilynn and I were sitting on the shoulders of the young men we had been drinking with. There is a two-page photo spread of that night in *Life Magazine,* and I've never figured out how we escaped being in that photo. I do think that would have shocked my parents. As it was, this so-called rioting did make the national news so finally my parents found out, too late, what going to Florida for spring break entailed.

    We had a merry time that evening until a ripple went through the crowd and somehow, somewhere, someone came up with the idea of rushing the pole and sweeping the policemen away in the crowd so that the fellow could escape. I had my feet on the ground by then, and it was extremely frightening to be moved along against one's will in the stampede. The guy I was with had his arm around me as we were suddenly confronted by a policeman wielding a billy club, who shouted, "Get her out of here!" I've tended to avoid crowds ever since.

    I also remember the night that I met an "older" man. This man was 28. I don't remember his name, but I do remember the snazzy red corvette convertible in which he drove me down A1A to Miami the next day to meet his family! Once we were with his parents it really wasn't much fun.

    All of us girls and several fellows from Illinois College went to Miami on Thursday evening as Marilynn's old boyfriend, Bob Stucker, threw a pool party for us at his parents' home. I drank too much that night, too, as I vaguely remember walking around the side of their house in the dark, tripping over a small wire fence and making a big crash into some bushes.

    We ate all of our meals at the Forum, a nice restaurant on the beach. In a letter I wrote to my folks after the trip, I estimated that we averaged $2 a day for food. I wrote, "That place was really nice to eat in. They had two dishes sitting on the table before you even ordered. Usually cole slaw & beets or cucumbers. Then, they gave you lots and lots of yummy rolls. The last two nights there we splurged and had big dinners. I had shrimp one time and some kind of fish the next night."

My share for gas going down to Florida was about ten dollars and coming back about five. We traveled back to Illinois College with Bob Stucker and his buddy in their car. It was a longer trip straight through from Fort Lauderdale to Jacksonville, Illinois, with six of us in a much smaller car. The boys didn't rotate drivers or stop to stretch like we girls had done on the way down. I remember being cramped and miserable.

I reported to my parents that "I didn't get very tan, I'm afraid. Barge & Marilynn were the ones who got the tans. I am a little browner, but not noticeable to anyone but myself. My hair is lighter from the sun & I have a few freckles—that's all."

I hate to admit that I was engaged at the time I took this trip. I wore my diamond on my right hand which really didn't fool anyone. I have no regrets that I went and that I did what I did for it broadened my horizons. The ratio of guys to girls at spring break in those years was 10 to 1 so I had never enjoyed so much male attention. I also met a greater variety of men from other parts of the country. Back at school, I became discontented and restless. The thought of being a housewife felt less desirable. I wanted to see more of the world. I wanted to meet more of those exciting men. In less than two months I had broken my engagement and broken a young man's heart. It wasn't an easy thing to do. I cried as much as he did. But it was the right thing to do. I've never regretted that I took that trip and went where the boys were.

About the Editor

Shari Wagner teaches poetry and memoir writing for the Writers' Center of Indiana. She is the author of *Evening Chore* (Cascadia, 2005), a collection of poems, and co-writer of her father's memoir about Somalia, *A Hundred Camels: A Mission Doctor's Sojourn and Murder Trial in Somalia* (Cascadia, 2009). Her poetry has been read by Garrison Keillor on *The Writer's Almanac* and has appeared in many literary magazines, including *North American Review, Black Warrior Review* and *Shenandoah*. Shari has received two Indianapolis Creative Renewal Fellowships and in 2009 was co-winner of *Shenandoah's* The Carter Prize for the Essay.

About the Photographer

James Todd has worked many different jobs. He has been a dishwasher, waiter, bartender, ballet dancer, actor, soldier in the Indiana National Guard and a sergeant on the Indianapolis Metropolitan Police Department. Since his recent retirement from the Police Department, he has been pursuing his interests in photography, music and writing.

In addition to taking the photographs for *Returning,* James served as a classroom volunteer for this memoir project, leading small group discussions.

About the Cover Designer and Photographer

Vienna Wagner is a freshman at Notre Dame and a graduate of Brebeuf Jesuit Preparatory School in Indianapolis. This is her second book cover project. She also created the Sufi-inspired mandala for the cover of her grandfather's memoir, *A Hundred Camels.*

Vienna's creative interests include photography, art and poetry. Her poem, "Art with a Heart," inspired by her afterschool work with students from Indianapolis Public Schools, was recently chosen for permanent display on a Mass Ave bus shelter as part of the Indianapolis Cultural Trail.

www.ingramcontent.com/pod-product-compliance
Lightning Source LLC
Chambersburg PA
CBHW032138040426
42449CB00005B/302